Dancing Through Life with Christ
How to Navigate a Relationship with an Invisible God

Michele R. Kenney

Cover by Lauren King

Copyright © 2017 Michele R. Kenney
All rights reserved.

ISBN-10: 154244130

ISBN-13: 978-1542441391

Dedications

This book is first of all dedicated to God. This was such a personal journey all the glory goes only to Him. Any benefit received from this book goes back to You Lord, do with it what you see fit.

My Thanks

First of all I want to thank God. Lord, you took me on this journey, you guided me every single step along the way. I asked for your guidance before I wrote each chapter, and I believe you responded. Thank you for this incredible journey. It was hard, but it was healing and on the other side of it I can say You are good. Your love endures forever. Though you slay me, yet I will praise you.

I want to thank my mom, Patti Kenney. Your support, not only in this book, but throughout my lifetime has helped mold me into who I am. You have and always will be my biggest cheerleader. Thank you for your guidance and advice throughout this process. I love you.

I want to thank my dad, Bob Kenney. You have been patient with my stupidity, and have never held it against me. I'm sorry, I love you. You have been a good example of God's enduring love for mankind.

My boys, Austin and Jordan Kenney. You boys have taught me more about God than anything else. Oh I love your wild spirits.

My Rick, you have influenced the person I am today more than you will ever know. You are whispered on the pages of this book. I hope someday you find the peace you long for. By the way, you are and always have been the baby bunny. I love you.

Thank you Lauren for creating the beautiful cover for this book. You are talented and did a great job. Jessie, you have been a good friend. Andrea, Thank you for being my friend. You are such a great listener, I love the times I am at the end of myself, and call you bawling my eyes out. You are patient with my ramblings.

Table of Contents

Introduction..5

Chapter 0
Reflection 7

Chapter 1
Dance With Me..9

Chapter 2
 Why Say Yes to the Dance with Christ.......15

Chapter 3
Dancing with Authenticity..........................23

Chapter 4
Dancing Through Shattered Dreams 45

Chapter 5
Dancing Through the Desert......................57

Chapter 6
Dancing in the Storm..................................71

Chapter 7
 Dead Man Dancing....................................77

Chapter 8
Dancing Among Wolves 87

Chapter 9
Dancing Against the Enemy.......................97

Chapter 10
When We Fall In the Dance 121

Chapter 11
Dancing Through Healing 129

Chapter 12
Dancing In His Grace 137

Chapter 13
Dancing the Dance of Hope 151

Chapter 14
Dancing Puzzle Pieces 163

Chapter 15
Dancing in Total Security 175

Chapter 16
Dancing In Freedom 183

Appendix I 189

Appendix II 193

Appendix III 201

Citations 207

Introduction

The day the idea of this book was conceived was a strange day for me. I was going for my normal run when the first flashes of this dream came into view. I had just led a DeColores weekend. My dancing themed approach to the talk about Total Security (based on chapter 4) was a hit, so I decided to write it down. That morning on my run the idea that I could actually write other chapters about dancing drifted through my mind. The idea started small and unsure, but by the end of my run I was ready. I had all kinds of ideas about the book. I would have a chapter about dancing with confidence, and one about dancing in victory, dancing with strength and one on perseverance. God was going to use me to give courage to his believers and I was pumped. Then everything changed…

After I wrote my first two chapters, and started on the third, which was supposed to be Dancing with Hope, I got a message on Facebook that flipped my world upside down. Without going into detail, this news sent my life violently spinning as if I were stuck in a tornado. For months it was all I could do to press on through life as I was faced with feelings, and realities I did not want to face. This changed the theme of my book completely. I had one agenda for this book, but God had another idea.

Writing this book has been one of the most incredible journeys of my life. It was hard and gut wrenching at times, but it pulled me into a deeper, more genuine relationship with God. Looking back I have no doubt the timing of the life changing event was meant to happen at the exact time that it did, if for no other reason than to rip open old wounds that needed to be healed, as well as to share that journey with you, my readers. This book is more than a book; it is my journey through the valley of the shadow of death. It is my heart laid bare. It is my road to healing. I hope you, my reader, will heal, grow and be changed by reading this book. To God be the glory.

"I want to sit at your feet, drink from the cup in your hand, lay back against you and breathe, feel your heart beat." ~Kari Jobe, The More I Seek You

"Listen in silence because if your heart is full of other things you cannot hear the voice of God." ~Mother Theresa

"Don't say God has been silent when your Bible has been closed" ~unknown

Chapter 0
Reflection

This is actually the last chapter I am writing. I realized at the end of my written work that I advise a lot about spending time with God, and gleaning from his word, however I do not go into any teaching about how you do that. I wanted to include one last chapter about dancing with Christ. So here it is. I guess I could call it Learning the Dance.

The first and most important step is silence. I go into some detail about this in the chapter Dancing with Authenticity. I cannot express to you enough how important it is to get alone, in silence with God on a regular basis. I don't have this down well, and I was reminded recently when a friend of mine told me, "That's your problem. You are so busy learning God's word, studying God's word, talking to God, and trying that you can't hear Him. When was the last time you sat in silence with him?" Quieting yourself before your maker is important.

Before I move on I want to give fair warning, it is not easy to be quiet before God. When I first began I was restless. I reached for my phone, I rushed the time, I wanted it to be over with. Becoming quiet before God is a learned behavior. Be patient with the process, and be patient with yourself. You will find the work and commitment worth it.

Next think of a subject you are struggling with. At least in the beginning this is a good way to "learn dance steps." If it is anger, look up Scriptures about anger. If it's gossip or a potty mouth look up verses about the tongue.

Write out the verses, and read each one several times. Begin to ask yourself and ask God what the verses mean. Ask yourself and God how you can actively apply what the verses are saying. Listen to what your heart, and what the Holy Spirit may be communicating to you.

Journal. Journal about what you are doing that goes against the Scripture. Journal about how you would like to do better. Journal about active plans and commitments on ways you will be able to do better. Journal about fears and obstacles making new changes.

These changes are hard. They require discipline, but Hebrews 12:11 speaks to that; "For the moment, all discipline seems painful rather than pleasant, but later it yields the peaceful fruit of righteousness for those who have been trained by it." Though learning these steps seem painful and hard in the beginning, you will find a relationship with God that is deep, and satisfying as a result.

"I cling to you; your strong right hand holds me securely." Psalm 63:8

"Show me your ways Lord, Teach me your paths." Psalm 25:4

"Won't you dance with me oh lover of my soul to the song of all songs." ~Jesus Culture; Dace with Me

Chapter 1
Dance With Me

When I was a child I loved to visit my grandparents in Baldwin, Michigan. It was a place of rest. They lived out in the middle of nowhere. Trees surrounded their home; there were no roads to the house only fire trails, which were made in case the trees caught on fire. It was beautiful, quiet, and peaceful.

I remember one year in particular, I was 13 years old, I had gone up there with my cousin, Tony, for a couple of weeks. One evening my grandparents decided it was time to teach us both how to dance. Grandma was my cousin's partner, and grandpa was mine. They taught us how to Waltz, Jitter Bug, Twist, and slow dance. We had a lot of fun that night; that is one of my fondest memories with them.

My grandpa instructed me by telling me that one key thing to dancing well is how the couple communicates with each other. Back when my grandparents were learning to dance it was not politically incorrect to assume that the man would lead, and the female would follow. It was the man's job as the leader to send his partner cue's to let her know what her next move was, and it was up to the woman to respond to those cue's. The more a couple danced together, the better she understood his cues and the easier it was for her to follow his lead. Another key thing my grandparents taught me is that there can only be one leader in a dance. When both partners try to lead it becomes a dysfunctional dance.

Christ asks all of us to dance the dance of life with him. It is his will that no one should perish. He asks us to dance with Him in different ways, but ultimately we are all asked.

There are different ways we may respond to his request to dance, but there is only one way that it goes well for us.

> #1 We may reject his request to the dance. Christ is a gentleman; he will not force us to do anything we don't want to do.

> #2 We may agree to dance, but as he is trying to teach us how to Waltz, we are too busy doing the Jitter Bug to even notice we aren't really dancing with him.

> #3 We may agree to dance with Christ, but then we try to lead him. This never works. He will not follow our lead.

> #4 We agree to dance with Christ, and we allow him to teach us new steps. This is when we learn to dance with beauty and grace. This is the only way we can rest peacefully in his arms. Dancing with Christ and allowing him to lead, is the only way to successfully dance through life.

I used to think this was a progression of our relationship with Christ, but over the years I recognize that there is a constant request from Christ to teach me new dance steps. There are still times he asks me to teach me something new yet I ignore him, I don't want to take that step, or I am too busy trying to do my own thing to cooperate. There are still times I try to lead him rather than follow his lead. But I have found that resting in his arms and allowing Christ to lead the dance of life is the only way to dance in this life with peace.

The thing about learning new dance steps is that it is a process. As with any other thing that I learn, it takes time to understand how to do those new steps right. Christ knows and understands that. He is a patient teacher. I may take the wrong steps, step on his feet, or trip myself up. But he is a gentle and loving teacher. He does not get mad when I get it wrong. He helps me learn and understand the new steps.

Notice in the above paragraph I said I might trip myself up. It's important to understand that we cannot trip up God. We trip ourselves up with choices we make but Scripture promises that God works all things together for good for those who love him and are called according to his purpose (Romans 8:28). Ultimately his will is done no matter what mistakes we make. You can see evidence of this through the story of Abraham in Genesis chapters 12-21.

So at this point you may be asking "How do I follow his lead? How do I know what steps he wants me to dance?" Glad you asked. Just as a dance partner gives his partner cues in a physical dance, God gives us cues in the spiritual dance through the Holy Spirit. They come in different ways. The cues may come by hearing the same truth over and over again. There have been times in my life where every sermon, every conversation, every song that came my way pointed to the same truth. That was a dance cue.

Sometimes it may come in a conviction. It may come in a quickening in your soul. When you hear something and immediately feel something in your soul responding, that is likely God saying to you "Listen up and respond." Sometimes it comes in that still small voice. It comes in your quiet times. Finding quiet time to sit and pray and study is always part of the dance. He cannot teach you new steps if you are not seeking him out and giving him your time. John 16:12-15 says that the Spirit speaks what He hears. We must put

God's truth into our own spirit in order that his Spirit may speak it back to us. The more we dig into the word of God, the more dance steps he will teach us.

Dancing Through The Fog

A word of caution: God can and will speak to some with visions, or in a distinctive voice, and even in the impressions we sometimes have, but always test the spirit. There is evidence that God communicated to his people through those means in the book of Acts, Daniel, Ezekiel, and Revelations among other books of the Bible, but be cautious about accepting anything apart from direct Scripture to be God. We have an enemy who is very real. He is out to steal your soul. One of his most powerful tools he has is deception. Recently I have come to the realization that he used that "still small voice" as a disguise. His deception kept me in a form of bondage for years.

Satan and all of his followers are spiritual beings, the same as God. They will try to deceive you by communicating to you, and they often use the same tools to accomplish their agenda. In 1 Timothy 4:1-2 we are told that in the later times there will be teachings that are taught by deceiving spirits. 1 Corinthians 11:14 says that Satan appears as an angel of light. Matthew 24:24 says that even the elect can be deceived. We must always be conscious to test any spirits or teaching against Scripture (1 John 4:1). If they don't line up with Scripture or God's revealed character, then it is not of God. It is also important for all of us to remain aware that our hearts are deceitful (Jeremiah 17:9). We can easily deceive ourselves into believing what we want to believe. It is so human to be easily led astray for candy-coated deception. One of the best dance steps to use when you are in the fog is to be still and wait for clarity and peace.

2 Timothy 2:26 says that just as God has a will for our lives, so does Satan. I am finding that there are times that God uses life to refine our character. But at that same time Satan takes the opportunity to lure us into his own will. When we are learning new dance steps

that are hard and painful the enemy of our soul begins to whisper to us about an easier way, he reminds us of our rights, or how we deserve better from God. Our flesh or our own desires can also appear as God. Again, we know how to deceive ourselves.

    I have been experiencing this in my own life as of recent. I have been faced with a situation that feels like it is full of ambiguity. There are times that God's will seems very cut and dry, there is no question what I am supposed to do, but that is not the case in this situation. There are complications in this situation such as my own desires that may deceive me, and of course the enemy of my soul. There are times I feel weak and tempted to do what I know is wrong, and there are times I feel confusion about what is right and wrong. This process is a step-by-step process where I cannot get ahead of God if I don't want to miss-step.

    Ultimately God is not apart from any difficult situation we find ourselves in. It is an opportunity for refinement of character. God has a will and a purpose for all things in our lives. It is in the midst of our struggles that he calls us into a deeper relationship with him. But the enemy of our soul also has a purpose in our struggles. If he can deceive us based on our desires he destroys the beauty that is meant to come out of our situations.

    Many blessings for God's future ministries and responsibilities for God's people rest on our ability to lean on his strength and follow his lead. God's will is to grow and prosper us; Satan's will is to cut us down in the process of our growth. Dance with Jesus long enough and you will dance through the fog. Dancing is learning to lean on your partner and learning to trust.

    We have no reason to fear our enemy, and we can rest assured that he does not have the ability to hear our thoughts as God can, but he can add to our thoughts. He has been studying mankind since the beginning, and he has been studying you from the beginning of your life. He knows your individual weaknesses and have no doubt, he can and will play on them. The enemy of our soul has had thousands of years to perfect his strategies. I can tell you based on my own life experience and mistakes how important it is that we always be on alert to be sure we are learning our dance steps from the right partner. We will talk in more detail about Satan in the chapter called Dancing Against the Enemy.

Dancing the dance with Christ is an exhilarating dance. He says he wants to give us life abundantly (John 10:10). His idea of abundantly living is different than ours, but it is definitely better. Whether you are already dancing the dance of life with Christ, or you have been asked to dance but you are unsure, this book has been written for you. I use my own experience as well as Biblical truth and my training in counseling to walk through dancing the dance of life with Christ.

Over the next few chapters we will look at reasons why we ought to dance with Christ, how to dance with authenticity, dancing through shattered dreams, the dance of hope, dancing in the desert, dancing through forgiveness and dancing in the waiting room along with other dances. I hope you find encouragement and answers to some things you may have questions to. So put on your dancing shoes and let's do a little jitterbug.

"Human history is the long terrible story of man trying to find something to make him happy." ~C.S. Lewis

"Why don't the names of Buddha, Mohammed, and Confucius offend people? The reason is that these others did not claim to be God, but Jesus did." ~ Josh McDowell

Chapter 2
Why Say Yes to the Dance with Christ

How do I know that Jesus is the right partner for me to dance with?

There are a lot of voices in the world inviting us to dance with them. There is the voice of Atheism, and voices of New Age, Eastern Practices, Islam, Wicca, Jehovah's Witness, and Mormonism to name a few of the popular ones in the United States. There are also voices that call out to us such as self-will, prestige, status, and wealth. All of these voices call out to us with the promise that they are the key to a good life. All of them are inviting us to dance with them. How do we know whose invitation we ought to accept?

Since the book you are reading is a Christian book the obvious conclusion I am going to give you is that Christ is the answer. But the next question to ask is why? Why not Islam? Why not self will? You may have already accepted the dance with Christ yet you still have questions. Before we go any further about how to dance the dance of life with Christ, I want to answer why dance the dance of life with him as well as how I know that he is the best partner in life. If you are not a fact person please be forewarned, the next two sections may be a bit dry for you, please hang in there anyway, it's a necessary part to establishing the foundation for the rest of this book. The chapter picks up again, I promise.

Is God a fairy tail?

There was a time when the existence of a god of some sort was not questioned. The bigger question was how many gods existed, who were they, and how do we keep them happy? Around about 1500-1700 A.D. man began to change his mind about God. Suddenly the question was not who is God, but rather is man god? As time progressed as well as man's accomplishments, the idea that man ought to be worshiped became more and more acceptable. The evolution theory only perpetuated the idea that there is no God.

I want to start my proposition that Christ is a good dancing partner by giving a brief overview of what my research has led me to conclude about the existence of a God. In the back of this book will be an extensive list of sources I have used both for support as well as against the idea that a God exists. I encourage everyone to explore the subject in depth on both sides.

Darwin with the help of Alfred Wallace and Jean-Baptiste Lamarck were the first to begin to put together the evolution theory. Of course, the advantage of proving there is no God frees us all from submitting to him, which allows us all to do as we please rather than what God commands. Darwin admitted there was one big obstacle to this theory and that was the Cambrian explosion.

The Cambrian explosion happened around what evolutionists theorize to be 543 million years ago. There was an "explosion" of new fossils that appear, but there are no links to prior species of these creatures. For over 150 years now evolutionists have looked for the fossils that show the gradual change between the fossils found in the Cambrian era, and the eras before, however nothing has been found.

This to me certainly is reason for question. If I decide one day to start searching my home for a Snicker's bar that is not there, I can search all I want, but since the fact remains one is not in my home, I will not find it. My determination does not make it real. Thousands of archaeologists have been looking for these links for more than 150 years, but they have not found any. If the fossils do not exist, researchers will not find any.

To further answer the question "is there a God", I must look to other facts. When Darwin came up with the evolution theory, the complexities of cells were not known. Even after so much technology, the complexity of the cell is still not understood. Many scientists have turned back to the idea that there must be intelligent design involved in the existence of this earth.

Next is the fact that some of the leading atheists and evolutionists, by their own admission, have holes in their theory. In his 2013 debate entitled "Life, the Universe, and Nothing", Dr. Lawrence Krauss admitted, "Science is getting closer to proving there is no need for a God for the beginning of the world to have happened." *(1) "Closer to proving there was no need for a God" still means there is no evidence to prove there was no need for a God for the universe to come into existence.

The evolution theory is nothing more than a theory; therefore it has not been proven as a fact. Let me clarify why this is significant; a theory is defined as a supposition or a system of ideas intended to explain something, especially one based on general principles independent of the thing to be explained. Where a fact is defined as a thing that is indisputably the case. Evolution is nothing more than a supposition, and has not had enough evidence to be considered a fact. The complexity of life, coupled with the holes in the theory of evolution tells me there is reason to believe that there is a God.

If there is a supreme being that designed me, it makes sense that he knows the intricacies of his creation. He is the author and designer of me, and he knows what is best for me. He is the one I am safest to dance with. The next question to ask is, "Who is that God?" There are many opinions.

How do I know Jesus is the Son of God?

I have heard people say that Jesus is a fictional character, like Tom Sawyer, or Sir Lancelot. But people who study history today have come to accept that Jesus of Nazareth did exist. There are certain criteria that must be met in order for anything to be accepted as historical evidence that supports that an event actually took place or historical figure really existed. Acceptable proof may be documentation of the event or written eyewitness accounts. For example we have no doubt that George Washington is a real historical figure because of the historical evidence that supports his existence. No one today ever met him, but we know that he lived because of the historical evidence that supports it. Also, no one today was alive when the Declaration of Independence was written or signed, but there is historical evidence to support that it was written and signed as a part of our American history, therefore it is still considered a legal document.

These forms of accepted historical documentation do exist in the case of Jesus of Nazareth and the events surrounding his life and death. Therefore it is not disputable that He existed. The question that needs to be asked is if he was who he claimed to be. In John 14:6 Jesus said, "I am the way the truth and the life no one comes to the Father but through me." This is an exclusive statement; meaning, if there is an ultimate supreme being that created the life of man, then Jesus claims to be the way to that source. Is he telling the truth? In the above statement Jesus not only claims to be telling the truth he claims to be the Truth.

C.S. Lewis, and Josh McDowell are two authors, among many, that have many interesting insights to this claim. Both educated men, both highly intelligent. If you want to explore this topic further I highly recommend them both. They both had agenda's when they approached the topic of the identity of Jesus Christ. Both men's agenda's were not to prove that he is the Son of God, but rather to prove he was not. McDowell was a law student who used his understanding of legalities and law to establish if there is reasonable evidence for belief in Jesus based on how court trials are investigated in criminal cases. For him, the study led to an undeniable understanding that Jesus was who he claimed to be and eventually McDowell accepted Christ as his Lord and Savior.

Now that I have established my reasons to believe there is an author of life, as well as my reasons to believe that Jesus is the connection to that author, let me move into why we benefit from dancing with him.

We all Thirst

Our society is determined to find happiness, and yet as I look around I do not see a society of happy people. I see many angry people who are short tempered. I see children who are being medicated for depression even though they have the latest iPhone, gaming system, 900 channels of television, and name brand clothes. I see people who are starving for love, yet they jump from unhealthy relationship to unhealthy relationship. According to an article in the New York Times**(2), more people are dying today as a result of suicide than as a result of car accidents. In addition 18.8 million adults in any given year will suffer from some form of depression**(3). Some professionals have gone so far to say that the rising trend of depression in this modern world is an epidemic. Why is this? If happiness is supposed to be achievable with every desire filled then why is it that in this world, where more people are achieving "the American Dream", suicide and depression is called an epidemic?

We all thirst, Scripture is clear on that. I found 26 Scriptures that were applicable to the thirst of the human soul, and my research by no means was extensive. But we often make the mistake of believing that we are thirsting for certain circumstances when in reality our thirst is for God.

At the beginning of time mankind was created to be in full communion to God. God walked in the garden with Adam and Eve, they enjoyed him, and he enjoyed them. Mankind was spiritually alive. We were meant to have the spiritual union with God from the day we were born. It was part of our design to be in unity with God. There was an automatic dance that was supposed to be going on between man and his creator. For Adam and Eve it came easy, it was functional and it was beautiful. That is the beauty our souls were created for; unity with God, our Father.

But there was an enemy of God lurking in the garden. He hates everything that God loves, and loves everything God hates. Since God loved man, man became the subject of Satan's wrath toward God.

In a vulnerable moment Satan planted a seed of doubt in the mind of Eve, the kind of doubt that doesn't trust God, the kind of doubt that desires to have control, the kind of doubt that resents God for trying to "control" us. That doubt has been passed down from generation to generation ever since. When Eve acted on her doubt, and then gave the forbidden fruit to her husband, the beautiful dance between God and mankind was broken. The spiritually alive part of man died and it stopped the automatic dance that was meant to be. This broken dance has left us thirsting for what we were made for.

Satan's biggest weapon still is deceit, he still twists the truth, and whispers doubt into our minds. "God wants to control me", "Religion is a bunch of rules meant to keep us from having fun", "Maybe we are all gods", "God is holding out on me, I deserve better". Because of these lies, many refuse to dance the dance of life with Christ, and many who do, still want to do it on their own terms.

Because of man's rebellion we are born into this world spiritually dead. The enemy of our soul, "the god of this world", also works to keep us blind from God (1 Corinthians 4:4). Beyond that, because of our own acts of rebellion God has handed us over to our lusts, and the unhealthy ways we try to quench our thirst (Romans 1:24-26; Ephesians 4:18-20). We were created to have unity with God, but human nature does not want to submit, we want to control our lives, we want control over how we quench our thirst, how to ease our longings. We want things our way, and we certainly don't want to hurt. Because of our rebellion against him, God allows us to be blinded from him. But there is hope to find our way back to God.

Jesus came to renew what was lost. Spiritual life does not come automatically, but it comes through the acceptance of Jesus Christ and from receiving the Spirit; you can learn more about this by reading the book of Romans. We must make the effort to seek God out. In Jeremiah 29:13 we are given the promise that when we seek him with all of our hearts he will be found. We find God when we accept Jesus; when we say yes to the dance with Christ. Jesus promises that when we come to him, he will quench our thirst through the Holy Spirit.

I used to wonder if Jesus promises a spiritual water that quenches our thirst why is it that I still thirst? I can drink deeply of him during my quiet times, but hours later I thirst again. I feel lack of strength, faith, security, or contentment. I truly believe that we will have some thirst until we get to heaven. In John 4 we read the account of Jesus interacting with a Samaritan woman. In this encounter he tells her that whoever drinks of the water he gives will never thirst again, however it is not until you read Revelation that you see Jesus giving his people the promised water.

But I also believe there is relief from our yearning here on earth. Here on earth I can drink deeply from my faucet in the kitchen, but a few hours later I get thirsty again. This is because I am in a physical world. I can drink water to quench my thirst, but it is only temporary. I must continually fill myself with water to stay healthy and to keep from being parched. I have even found there are days that I remain thirsty to some extent no matter how much water I drink, so too for our spiritual thirst. There is an element of spirituality here on earth, yet we are still in a physical world. Therefore we have to make a constant effort to stay "hydrated" in him, and sometimes we thirst for more of him no matter how deeply we drink.

We find some degree of quenching our thirst by seeking out his word, and by being real with him. We must first come to Christ, and then pour out our longings to him. Trust him. So many times Christians do not pour out their longings. They keep them hidden, even from themselves. It is so important for us to go, vulnerable to the feet of Jesus and cry out about our frustrations, disappointments, grief, and aches. Through the Spirit, we can find relief and strength to press on in spite of those aches because he fills us up. We must fill up on the Word of God daily. God will pour truth into our life through Scripture and we pour it out through our action in daily life.

    Some Christians have put on a false sense of guilt because they thirst, long, or yearn. But here on this earth we will thirst. When going through tough times I may thirst for relief from my pain. What determines sinfulness is what I do with my thirst, longings, and yearnings. Do I reach for my drug of choice, which can be anything from illegal drugs to an excess of food, or an over the top shopping spree. It may be indulging in pornography, or some other behavior that is unpleasing to God, yet pleasing to the flesh. Or do I determine to take my thirst to the feet of Jesus and sit in the discomfort as I wait on him.

    In this world, we may find a very temporary relief by indulging in those things the flesh cries out for, but soon afterwards we find ourselves aching stronger than ever before. Eventually the aching leads to slavery. Quenching your thirst by anything other than Christ leads to bondage (Romans 6:8; Galatians 4:8-9). Bondage causes more thirsting. It is hard to sit in discomfort and wait quietly on God, but it is the only way to truly deal with our thirst and find some relief. Many of us do not exercise the patience for this. We live in a society that demands all longings to be met now, but there are no quick fixes when it comes to spirituality. Sometimes we have to wait a while for Jesus to come and quench our spiritual thirst. We don't always understand why we must wait so long for him, or know how long we will have to wait, but one thing is for sure, nothing fills up the soul of a human being like Jesus can. What better reason is there to say yes to the dance with him?

    Now that we have covered why we should say yes to the dance of life with Christ, let's begin to explore some of those dances.

---

*(1) Sourced in the appendix and in the back
**(2)(3) Sourced in back

"Learn to see yourself as you are and accept your weakness until it pleases God to heal you." ~Francois Fenelon

"When hints of sadness creep into our soul, we must not flee into happy or distracting thoughts. Pondering the sadness until it becomes overwhelming can lead us to a deep change in the direction of our being from self-preservation to grateful worship." ~ Dr. Larry Crabb

"Painted on, Life is behind a mask. Self inflicted circus clown, tired of the song and dance. Living a charade, always on parade. What a mess I've made of my existence." ~Natalie Grant; Real Me

"She's one of the walking wounded the bleeding doesn't show, Behind the wall around her heart, where none's allowed to go." ~Don Fransisco; Walking Wounded

Chapter 3
Dancing with Authenticity

In Christian circles, there is a lot of talk about the freedom we find in Christ, yet it is my belief that many of us don't walk around with much freedom. There may be freedom to some degree and we put a lot of attention on those areas yet, we try to stuff the other areas where we feel less free. How many of us know we are free from condemnation from our past, so we focus on that version of freedom, yet we still struggle with feelings that are deemed unacceptable in the Christian world such as disappointment or depression. I know that I have found myself battling with feelings that I am ashamed to admit to in front of other believers because of the pressure in those types of areas. I have found myself faking it and somehow I get the feeling that I am not the only one.

For years I have struggled with a disappointment that goes so deep I can't begin to express it to you in words. I knew God was taking me in one direction, when I wanted to go in another. I was obedient to him, but in my obedience I had expectations of how things should turn out. My hopes for my future did not happen. I did my best to put my disappointment and grief on the shelf. As any good Christian, I looked to Scripture to help with my attitude. I prayed Scriptures out loud to help "Trust in the Lord with all of your heart and lean not on your own understanding" (Proverbs 3:5-6). "Lord, please be delighted with the meditations of my heart and the words that I speak" (Psalm 19:14). "God works all things together for those who love him and who are called according to his purpose" (Romans 8:28).

I was self-controlled with my words. I tried to keep my thought process pleasing and pure. I tried to speak the words of truth and to ignore my hearts cries. Every now and then the cries got so over whelming I had to speak my heart ache to my mother, best friend, or sometimes even to God. I would confess repent and then go back to sucking it up. I tried my best to be a good Christian girl. I was playing the role I was expected to play. But without fail it would build until the burden was once again too heavy for me to carry and I would have to let it out again. Every time this happened, I tried to let just enough out to relieve my grieving heart, but it was never fully relieved.

What choice did I have? God said "no" to my heart's desire. There is much I don't understand because his ways are higher than mine (Is. 55:8-9). So I kept my disappointments as close to myself as possible. I slapped a great smile on my face and trusted God. And then one day God said, "Enough!! Enough faking; enough pretending. Enough playing a religious good girl role. You are putting distance between you and myself and it is keeping you from being the woman I created you to be. You have stunted your own growth in my name and it is time we put an end to your pious pretenses."

There was a triggering event that brought it all to the surface, but that was God's surgical tool that cut open the infected wound inside my heart. At the same time this was going on, my son had a staph infection, the infection had to be cut out of his back. He was awake during this outpatient minor surgery and it hurt him bad. It was hard for me, as his mama to watch him go through it, but we both knew there was no way around it. The infection had begun to affect the healthy tissue all around his original wound and the only way to get his body to heal was to cut it out. I realized that God did the same thing to my heart. The disappointment, depression, pain that I refused to face was affecting other areas in my heart as well. The only way to get healing to happen was to cut out the infected areas.

After my son's minor surgery, puss continued to ooze for days as deeper infection worked it's way out. The same process happened with me. After God began to cut and scrape (and may I say there was actual physical pain that came with this spiritual surgery) I continued to ooze for weeks. But with the discharge came relief.

My "infection" oozed to the point that secret feelings I had kept from most people for years began to come out. At first I told only a few people what I was struggling with, but my pain got so intense that I didn't care who knew, or if they kept my "sinful struggle" a secret. I am human. I was horrified by what I found in my own heart. I also realize that if the truth be told, if I were able to take an honest look at anyone else's heart, I would be horrified by what they wrestle with too. We all have ugliness in our hearts, no matter how fervently we seek God. Paul himself, the man who wrote ¾ of the New Testament admits he continued to struggle to do what is right, and he claimed to be the worst of all sinners (Romans 7:15; 1 Timothy 1:15-16). Well then me too, and I am no longer too proud to admit it.

During the process, I felt like Princess Elsa from the Disney Movie Frozen. For years out of fear she locked herself away. She needed to be good, and controlled so she played a role for everyone else's sake. It was a role that she knew she was expected to play. But it was not true to who she was. She was not allowed to feel what she felt, or be who she was. Acting incongruent with who she was put a lot of pressure on her. Christians also frequently play a role that is incongruent with what they feel and it puts a lot of pressure on us. The thing that is sad is that often times Christians create an environment that puts this kind of pressure on each other too.

Elsa's secret that she had been hiding from everyone caused a big mess when it came out into the open. She is ridiculed and misunderstood and so she runs away to be herself. While she is running away to isolation she sings the song "Let it Go". The words are appropriate to how I was feeling as I finally embraced the feelings I had been hiding for so long.

"…A kingdom of isolation and it looks like I'm the queen.
The wind is howling like this swirling storm inside.
Couldn't keep it in, Heaven knows I tried.
Don't let them in, don't let them see
Be the good girl you always have to be
Conceal don't feel don't let them know
Well now they know
Let it go let it go!
Can't hold it back anymore
Let it go, let it go
Turn away and slam the door.
I don't care what they're going to say
Let the storm rage on
The cold never bothered me anyway."

I can't help but wonder how many other Elsa's we have in the "Christian" world. How many Christians are too afraid to admit that they struggle with trusting in a God they cannot see or feel. How many struggle because it would be horrible to admit out loud that they are struggling to be content with who they are married to? How many people understand that God is unpleased with homosexuality, yet they can't make those feelings they have toward the same sex leave? How many Christians struggle with depression, yet they know the stigma within the church when it comes to depression? How many people resent others in the church, they try to lay their sinful feelings at the cross, but there are people who just rub them raw emotionally?

Maybe the struggles aren't even as difficult as the one's I named above. Perhaps it is just that there is disappointment with God, anger, or a lack of trust. How many of us hide our true feelings behind Scripture? We quote the truth out loud because Christ is truth, and we are free in his truth. Right? So we just pretend, we don't really allow ourselves to feel what we are feeling.

But there are other truths that interfere with holding steadfastly to the truth of Christ. How we are truly feeling can get in the way of accepting the real truth of Christ at the level we need to. We may have the head knowledge of Christ's truth, but an honest look at our emotions shows we are struggling with grasping God's truth. The turmoil may be based on lies, or lack of faith, or real pain. It doesn't matter what the cause of the pain, the pain is real and cannot always be ignored. That is when we need the courage to wrestle through it, not the cowardice to hide behind a religion. Our emotions will not change to a firmer faith by ignoring them.

Though many Christians may not agree with me on this subject, I believe there is much truth to what I have to say on this. Not because I am such a great theological expert, but I believe God gave me a lesson in it as He began to heal my own frozen heart.

When I was struggling through the situation I wrote about earlier, I had many people try to tell me their idea of "truth" on the subject. One person said, "I don't believe for a moment this is from God. Just keep praying against Satan and God will make the situation different than it ever has been." But as I searched Scripture what I found did not agree with my friend. What I found is that I am promised tough times and disappointment.

Another person told me, "Do not ever speak that struggle out loud again. You are giving the enemy weapons to use against you. You speak God's truth out loud only. Those other things are just emotions and you can't trust emotions. Speak what you want enough and your emotions will follow."

My problem with what she said to me is that my struggle was genuine. It was real. I had spoken Scriptural truth for years, but the truth of my pain and disappointment stayed in my heart. I had ignored my feelings and rarely spoke it out even to God but this strategy wasn't getting me anywhere. Don't get me wrong, I agree that we can't fully trust emotions, but we can't totally discount them either. I can agree that I feel many things emotionally that are based on lies. But I also know sometimes emotions are trustworthy. Furthermore God gave us our emotions; they are a gift and should not to be feared. Emotions do need to be kept in the right place, just as food is a gift that can be abused, so can the gift of our emotions be abused. There is an important balance that we must find.

The other problem I had with what my friend said is, nowhere in Scripture does it say for me to be careful about speaking my heart out of fear of the enemy. In fact, quite the opposite is Scriptural. Here are some of the Scriptures I found against her theory:

> *Is. 54:17 "No weapon formed against me shall prosper."*
> *Psalm 23:4 "I will fear no evil."*
> *Psalm 27 "The Lord is my light and salvation whom shall I fear…though war break out against me even then will I be confident."*
> *1 John 4:4 says "Greater is he that is in me than he that is in the world."*

There are other Scriptures I could use to back up that I have nothing to fear when it comes to spiritual warfare, these are just a few. I see no support to be afraid to speak my heart. But I do see support to be transparent about my emotions. As I weighed my own thoughts, and experiences against Scripture on this subject, I tried to find Biblical references on how to handle emotions, transparency, genuineness, authentic, feelings, and truth. I couldn't find much directly addressing these subjects. I looked up Greek, and Hebrew definitions on some of these to see what I could find. I still came up with nothing directly. Truth in Scripture almost always points to Christ himself. Though the truth of Christ is absolutely relevant, it didn't quite get to the core of what I was searching for. What I did instead was look to Biblical accounts of people who had recorded episodes of despair, depression, anxiety, and other forms of struggle; this is what I found:

- Job spoke his death wish out loud in Job 6:8-10 and in Job 7:11 He spoke about his anguish
- David spoke his feelings of abandonment and disappointments out loud in Psalm 75.
- In most of Ecclesiastes, but particularly 2:17-22, Solomon spoke his feelings of disillusionment. He goes as far to say he hated life and all things in it because it is all meaningless.
- In Mark 9:24 the Centurion spoke his lack of faith out loud to Jesus Christ and asked for help overcoming it.
- In 1 Kings 19 Elijah, like Job, told God he had enough of life, and asked God to end it.

When Lazarus died, though Jesus knew what was coming next he cried with Mary and Martha. I have heard some say that he cried because of their lack of faith. I don't see where Scripture backs that up. I believe this idea must be based on speculation. What I do see in this Scripture Jesus was moved to the point of weeping with his friend. I believe it is possible that Jesus grieves with us when we are grieving. He hears our laments (Psalm 56:8) and he promises to wipe away every tear (Revelation 21:4). This does not reveal a God who grieves by our expressions of emotions, or who becomes angry or disappointed in us when we are not constantly resting in him. It shows a God who cares when we shed tears.

I know I am not the only one who has studied the character of God who has come to this conclusion. In the book When Life and Beliefs Collide; How Knowing God Makes a Difference*(1) the author Carolyn James says of the circumstances surrounding the resurrection of Lazarus, "But the simplest explanation (which is almost always the best one) is that Jesus weeps for Mary. He weeps with her over the loss of her brother and his dear friend. He weeps for her because she is confused, and he knows how hard it is for her to understand him. He weeps because she suffers. His tears tell us that our pain is real and he will never minimize it."

In Genesis 32:22-32 Jacob wrestled with God. We are not told details about how the angel of the Lord came or exactly why, but we are told that Jacob had made some poor choices that led to conflict with his father in law and also with his brother Esau. At this point in the story, Jacob was literally surrounded with consequences to his poor choices. His father in law had been chasing him on one side of a brook. God intervened and saved his life, only for Jacob to find out his brother, who had wanted to kill him, was on the other side of the brook coming to meet him. Jacob had caused a mess for himself. That night Jacob wrestled God until dawn. In the end God won, but not before touching the socket of Jacob's hip. Jacob walked away with the scars from wrestling with God, but he was blessed for having the courage to wrestle with Him.

I have been told that when we wrestle with our emotions it is always our lack of faith, and it is a sin issue. According to some when we wrestle with God it is evidence that we have taken our eyes off of Jesus. This may be true at times, but I don't believe it is always true. Grief is a genuine emotion. Grief over the loss of a loved one, or over the loss of a dream, or over betrayal is not sinful. And what about wrestling over something God wants us to do when we don't want to do it?

I was so blessed when I was reading Hebrews just a few days ago and came across Hebrews 5:7-9 which says,

> *"During the days of Jesus' life on earth, he offered up prayers and petitions with loud cries and tears to the one who could save him from death, and he was heard because of his reverent submission (notice he was heard, yet he still went to the cross) Although he was a son, he learned obedience through what was suffered."*

Not only were Jesus' pleas not sinful, but also he was heard for his reverent submission. He cried. He pleaded and he was God. We are allowed to cry and plead when we are hurting too. We are allowed to wrestle out loud with God and be authentic with him. We must remain obedient, but our reverent submission is appreciated and honored by God.

An authentic relationship with Christ only comes when we are authentic or genuine with him. Not by hiding from ugliness we hold in our hearts. I have a friend who lost his only child. For years he refused to watch commercials with children in it, hold a child, watch children play baseball, or even be in a nursery. He also ignored God. He was hiding. By the way healing did come when he stopped hiding.

I heard of a Christian servant who loved the Lord. He touched many people with his famous talent of ministry. But one day he shocked the Christian community when he joined the homosexual community. He had tried stuffing his feelings for so long, he couldn't pretend anymore. To this day it is my understanding that he remains living in rebellion to God.

When I came to the end of my pretending I had to stop saying to myself and everyone else "All is as it should be and I am so blessed." When I read my journals from this era it is so guarded. My prayers even sounded fake. Authentic meant I had to tell God, "I trusted you in this, I felt like I deserved a different outcome, and quite honestly I am angry at you. I don't trust you anymore. I have these sinful feelings in my heart, I'm tired of pretending they aren't there, I can't get rid of them, I'm sinful and I have no idea how to change it." To be genuine means you stop hiding parts of yourself that you don't want to face.

I can hear the protests of those who disagree already. "What? Is she saying a homosexual is to embrace their feelings or an adulterer should face the fact they want to commit adultery with someone? This is the false teaching Timothy 4:3 spoke about." But before you get too carried away with your judgment, please let me finish my thoughts.

> Psalm 139:1-3 says,
> *1 "Oh Lord you have searched me and you know me.*
> *You know when I sit and when I rise; you perceive my thoughts from afar.*
> *You discern my going out and my lying down*
> *You are familiar with all my ways."*

According to Scripture God knows those deep down feelings. He knows if you are struggling with homosexuality, thoughts of adultery, mistrust, anger at him, a demanding heart, or an unloving spirit. Whether it is right or wrong, he knows exactly what is in your heart and what you are struggling with. Why hide it?

> 1 John 3:18-20 says:
> *18"Dear children let us not love with words or tongue but with actions and in truth. 19This then is how we belong to the truth, and how we set our hearts at rest in his presence 20 whenever our hearts condemn us. For God is greater than our hearts and he knows everything.*

If we are truly following after Christ, we can put our hearts at rest in spite of our sinful thoughts, or longings. Because God judges everything based on the truth and He is greater than our flawed hearts. He knows the truth is that we cannot fully shed off our sinful ways. Our thoughts will continue to be selfish, our hearts will continue to be discontented, we may always have flair ups of jealousy. And God knows that. He recognizes that we have not made it to our transformed perfected selves yet. We expect more from ourselves and from each other than God expects from us. We judge ourselves and each other by what we think we know, God judges us based on truth. We are flawed sinners, and we have all been saved by his grace and mercy. We all have sinned and fallen short of the glory of God (Romans 3:23). We all do what we don't want to do, and we refuse to do the good we know we ought to (Romans 7:14). God has mercy on us anyway.

I believe that Scripture takes this a little further even. Psalm 139 says "You knit me together in my mother's womb. I am fearfully and wonderfully made." I believe that God intimately knows the flaws we struggle with. In some cases he knows our greatest strengths will also be our greatest weaknesses. Natural gifts God gives us can get us in a lot of trouble until we learn how to let God have them.

Please don't misunderstand what I am saying about being authentic or genuine here. I don't mean to imply that embracing your struggle means to indulge in it. There is a difference. Embrace the depression, embrace your grief, embrace your disappointment or lack of faith or the sin you struggle with. Acknowledge that it is there; be honest about your story to whomever you need to be honest with. Go on whatever journey you may need to go on to process your disappointment, grief, and anger. Don't ignore it, wrestle through it with God. But do it with a clear conscience. Don't indulge in sinful behavior as you journey through the pain.

Depending on the journey, you may be tempted to do things that clearly go against Christian living. But indulging in your temptation is not the same as facing it. Scripture is clear that you cannot know Christ and continue to sin (Rom. 6:1-2; 1 John 3:6-10). We crucify our flesh in order to follow Christ; we do not indulge in it

(Gal.5:24). There is a beautiful balance we need to find as we deal with ugliness in our hearts. Avoiding what is genuine in our hearts because it is too painful, or scary is equally as sinful as indulging in it. Lewis Smedes says it well in his book Sex for Christians*(2) where he points out that we are to stay away from idols. Idols are those things we avoid out of fear as much as they are things we fall down to worship.

Healing only comes when we face those things we wrongfully worship (or fear) head on and take them to the feet of Jesus.

When we ignore raw emotions it is usually out of self-protection. But here is the problem with self-protection; we close off parts of ourselves, thus changing our hearts. If my friend has hurt me in certain areas, and I close myself off to him in those areas out of determination to never be hurt by him again, I selfishly changed my heart to protect myself. If I leave one church that has hurt me, and begin to attend another church determined to stay away from the same situations that hurt me previously, I isolate myself and change a part of my heart. If I am hurt because I prayed about something and it appears that God did not show up, and in response I begin to withdraw from God in that area, I have distanced myself from God. I have withdrawn a part of my heart to protect myself.

No matter the situation, self-protection changes one's heart. Out of the overflow the heart the mouth speaks (Matt 12:34; Luke 6:45) As I change my heart to protect myself, soon my actions will follow. The bottom line is that as I change to protect myself, I also change the heart God created me to have, all in the name of safety. Even as I am writing this, may I confess to you I don't have self-protection mastered? In some ways it still masters me. I am aware of it, and I continue to wrestle with it before God. But I am brave enough to wrestle.

It is important to understand that wrestling with God, or being genuine before him does not guarantee full healing, or answers to every question you have. There are questions I may take to my grave. There are pains I may carry throughout my life. The disappointment I was faced with that I wrote about earlier in this chapter has shifted during my wrestling match with God, but it has not resolved. Honestly, I doubt it ever will be fully resolved but I have a healthier relationship with it than I once did. There are no promises with the outcomes when you are genuine before Christ. What can happen when you are genuine with God is that you have the chance to grow in character, integrity, and strength. You have the opportunity to experience God's character in a new way and you will possibly see things from His perspective more than you ever have before.

As I wrestled my way through the ugliness of my disappointments, I saw life differently. But I also felt the Holy Spirit offering me strength to get through the pain. I grew in ways I cannot explain in words. God showed up in my tailspin. He was my "shalom peace within the storm". He revealed himself to me in ways he had not before.

God stripped away some of my false thinking I had about him, and about hope. He revealed to me that I had once again constructed my own version of God. We should not put God into a box, or hold onto a false hope, when we do we are fashioning an idol—a false version of God. God is the God that he is-period.

In C.S. Lewis' book the Lion the Witch and the Wardrobe the Lion*(3), Aslan is representative of Jesus Christ. The character Beaver begins to tell the 4 children who come to visit Narnia about Aslan as they ask questions about him, Beaver says to them, "Safe…who said anything about safe? Course he isn't safe. But he is good. He's the King I tell you." I have a greater understanding of this statement than ever before. God doesn't shield us from disappointments or pain. He doesn't break us down and then build us back up the way we want him to, but his character remains good. We can have faith in his goodness and his faithfulness even as we lose faith in all the things we believe about him.

Through my episode, I also felt like God gave me a small glimpse of how he views humanity. The longing he feels for those who have rejected him. The longing he feels as he looks upon those that he knows will never accept his love. How he feels as he loves us so purely and genuinely, and yet we lack understanding of that love. We say we love him, but we have no idea what his version of love really is. I feel like I better understand the longing he has to protect us from ourselves, even as we insist on doing things our own way.

I have experienced acting out the patience of perfect timing, and the understanding of when to move and when to silently allow things to play out. I am not saying I see things exactly as God sees them, but over the last few months I felt like I got a glimpse of Gods feelings.

God longs for us "Jerusalem, Jerusalem, you who kill the prophets and stone those sent to you, how often I have longed to gather your children together, as a hen gathers her chicks under her wings, and you were not willing"(Luke 13:34). God feels anger, even though He is slow to it (Exodus 32:11, Isaiah 5:25; Psalm 103:8). God is compassionate and loving (Numbers 14:18; Psalm 145:8). I believe sometimes he uses our emotions in the tough times to help us to relate to his own emotions.

One thing about being genuine, it takes courage to invite Christ into the struggles of your heart. Again, Christ is a gentleman. He will not come into the situations uninvited. You must be willing to see your feelings for what they are and admit them. Then you must be willing to invite him to do his surgery. It hurts and it isn't easy, but God is faithful to those who are willing to take the chance with Him.

The Other Kind of Genuine

I have spent much of this chapter focused on how we can dance an inauthentic dance with Christ by avoiding our feelings of disappointment, depression, anxiety, anger, lack of faith and other feelings that we find uncomfortable, but that is not the only dance of inauthenticity we can dance. We find an example of another dance of inauthenticity VS. The dance of true genuine-ness in Luke 18:9-14 where Jesus tells a parable specifically to address some people who were confident of their own righteousness, yet looked down on others who seemed less holy than them.

The parable is about two men who go to the temple to pray. The first, who is a Pharisee, looks up to heaven with great confidence and begins to pray about his greatness. "God, I thank you that I am not like other men--robbers, evildoers, adulterers—or even this tax collector who is next to me. I fast twice a week, and give a tenth of all I get."

This Pharisee made a big scene, and he made sure to praise himself. I don't know that very many Christians in today's society would make the same type of scene about their holiness. We know too much about grace in our generation to be that blatant with our arrogance. Our society tends to be a little subtler in our self-righteousness.

Recently, I was at a dinner where an honored guest first prayed over the meal, but then said to everyone, "I like to go last, my wife knows that about me, anyone who knows me well knows that I go last. You all go first, and I will take what is left." As the dinner continued he went table to table making sure everyone at every table knew that he was humble enough to let every guest go before he, the honored guest. This was an obvious example of false humility. I don't mean to pick on him; if I am honest I have been guilty of building myself up to be holier than I am too.

I love to go through my Bible and highlight, circle and make notes in the margins. My dogs, for the last 3-generation of doggies have all chewed a little more off my leather cover. The pages on my Bible are dog eared and well worn, full of highlights, underlining, notes and spilled coffee from years of use. I have to be honest, I have been guilty of feeling a sense of pride at times when I pull out my much loved Bible at a Bible study for everyone to see what a dedicated studier I am. And I always feel disappointment if the address of the Scripture is in some neglected book like Obadiah or Zephaniah where I am lucky to have one small sentence underlined because I've not thoroughly studied the book.

Are the honored guest from above and myself the only ones who at times dance the dance of inauthenticity? We feel as though we must build up the case of our holiness for others to see. Or maybe it's for God to see. But really all we do is fool ourselves. How many of us have gone through seasons where we feel like Sunday morning services are redundant. We have heard these Scriptures we get the truth mostly, so there is little more we need to learn.

How many of us have felt the need to share what God is doing with the ministries he has entrusted us with, yet our motivation for sharing is more to let others know how important we are to God? I know I have felt that was the motive of many people as they talk up how God uses them…if I'm honest I have been guilty of the exact same version of pride.

I can't help but wonder how God feels about our audacity to puff ourselves up as we take credit in our ability to follow him so well. The reality of our condition is that we are all at His mercy. We are all still full of sin. Sure we are new creations, sure old things are passed away, but we will never truly walk in perfection until the day we have our new transformed bodies. Try as we do to minimize our lack of perfect love for our spouse, our inability to be patient in every single scenario, our inability to always keep our minds pure, to never pass judgment on others, we will continue to fall short. God knows this, and understands it, which is why he went to the extreme to send his son to die for the reconciliation of us to him.

When we put our heart's condition into perspective we have no choice but to fall down at the feet of Jesus and confess we are full of pride and we need him to keep us in true genuine humility. We need him to give us a genuine understanding of who we are and to remind us of our dependence on him.

May I just throw something out here that I feel is worthy of mentioning? I have been absolutely horrified by some of the things I have seen posted by Christians in the name of Christ on Facebook. For example, hours after a famous actor committed suicide some people were posting things that may have been "truth", but it was harmful truth for the moment. The posts were about depression, and suicide, and how we should not be honoring this man's life because of the sinful way he died. I have seen people posting on Facebook their own judgments of whether people are going to heaven or hell. But Romans 2:1-4 and James 2:12 both say it is not our place to pass judgment, whenever we do, we claim to have the purity and the understanding that belongs to only God.

I don't pretend to know where any individual will land in the spiritual after life. But even further, divisive statements thrown out in the public eye will only harm the kingdom of God. We must be very careful to keep our holiness connected to genuine humility. There is a time and a place to speak harsh truth, and speaking to a grieving community that someone who is loved is in hell is not a wise time. I wonder how many non-believers took some of these posts as one more example that Christians are insensitive and judgmental. Instead, grieving at the pain this actor must have felt to drive him to such a drastic act could be appealing to those who don't know Christ. I'm certain I have been guilty of such insensitivities without realizing it, but I pray that God helps me to always show compassion first, and give me wisdom when to speak and when to keep my mouth shut.

The above was an example of Christians showing the self exalting, inauthentic holiness to the world, but I believe sometimes we can show great compassion to those who are in the world, yet get self righteous with fellow Christians. We see someone else facing a tragedy we have never been faced with, but we judge the way they handle it. Or we compare their holy life to ours to see how we measure up to them, or how they measure up to us. I am ashamed to say there have been moments I have celebrated to myself when someone didn't handle things the way I deemed correct. What a false way to live the Christian life. I build my props all around me to help me feel better about my righteousness. All of it is evidence of being phony.

The parable goes on. The other man who came into the temple to pray was a tax collector. He stood at a distance from the others. He would not even lift his head out of his shame and humility. He beat his breast and said "God have mercy on me, a sinner."

This man did not compare himself to others who were worse sinners (there always will be someone you can perceive as worse than you), he did not focus on his good deeds, or areas where he has things right. He was honest that he was not worthy of God, and he understood the forgiveness he needed was dependent upon God's mercy. This is where all Christians need to be, regardless of where we are in our walk with Christ. We are never holier than anyone else. We are all in need of God's mercy and grace on a daily basis.

The end of the parable, Jesus points out that it was the second man whose prayers were accepted by God, not the first man's. When we need to exalt ourselves we have received our reward, but we will face a time when God will humble us. But if we humble ourselves, we will be exalted.

The dance of being genuine, begins with recognizing your true feelings, and ends with embracing how ugly your heart really is. No matter how pure your heart gets, no matter how refined you become in Christ, there are still areas where you lack purity and understanding. The beauty of it is you are not alone. Have you ever been around someone who always has to be right? Have you ever been around a person who is deemed to be an expert on a certain subject, but who seems open to learning or hearing what others have to say? Who do you have more respect for the person who is always right or the one who quietly takes in more than he speaks?

I don't mean to drag politics in this book, but the story is relevant. There was a controversial president who made some choices that caused a great deal of criticism and division in this country. To add to the turmoil this president faced there was a documentary (based on lies) that was compiled through the presidency. He faced a lot of ridicule. I always liked this president, but a friend of mine, on the other hand, bought into much of the propaganda. I stuck to my beliefs that he had good character. On the night before his successor's inauguration, this president stood before America and "ate crow." He admitted that perhaps he made some choices that he should not have. He said as he looked back there were a few things he would do differently if he could, but throughout his presidency he always did what he thought was best for the nation at the time, and he can look himself in the mirror everyday knowing that he did his best everyday, even if it wasn't always flawless. That night, this president won the respect of my friend.

It is human to wrestle with life; it is human to mess up. If God doesn't condemn you for being flawed, why do we have such a hard time embracing it about ourselves? Why are we so quick to condemn each other? Isn't it time we get real with ourselves and with God? After all, he knows if we are being real or not anyway.

Only Jesus can help with your sin issues; he can help with your emotional issues. Is it time for you to invite him into areas of your heart that you have been holding back from him? Is it time for you to become truly authentic with God?

Learning to be authentic can be difficult, and it is even harder in a world as full of noise as our world is today. We have so many distractions that we don't know how to quiet ourselves. Many of us may have never gotten quiet enough to know who we authentically are. It is easy to hide from our ugly feelings. So many people today don't even know what they are thinking or why, they just act. It can be difficult to learn how to change that. Let me help you. Pretend I am there with you, in your living room, or bedroom, or wherever you may be. Let me teach you how to find your authentic self.

> Start by turning off all distractions. All televisions, music, put your phone on silent and put it out of your reach. If you are in a house full of people, go off to a room all by yourself. Find a closet if you must.

Next get comfortable. Close your eyes and let go of all agenda's, worry of things that you need to get done and time. Just rest and breathe. This may be hard to do, but do it anyway; it will get easier as you learn to rest quietly before God.

Become aware of yourself. Turn your focus inward to your body. Feel your tension in your body, feel your emotions, become aware of your thoughts. Become aware that God loves you, and is present with you right now. Be aware that he wants to hear from you.

Don't push uncomfortable feelings away. Feel the full weight of them. Be compassionate with yourself, and know that God is compassionate to you too.

Pray. Psalm 139 says, "Search me and know my heart Oh Lord. See if there is any offensive way in me." You could say that Scripture or you may simply pray and ask God to search your heart and help you connect with anything you are hiding from. Ask God to bring to your mind anything that needs to be dealt with.

Continue to allow yourself to feel, and listen to what your mind brings forward.

Invite Jesus into these situations and emotions.

Begin to talk to Jesus about what you are experiencing. Don't hold back. Don't be afraid to be honest. Don't be afraid to fall apart.

Know that Jesus is tenderly holding your emotions, no matter what they are.

Stay in the moment as long as you need to.

Make a decision to trust God with every emotion you poured out to him.

Repeat as often as you need to.

Be patient with yourself.

Know that this may be awkward at first, if nothing happened the first time, keep trying. Eventually you will feel confident with this.

If you were struggling, it may also help to bring Scripture into this time. One good Scripture may be Matthew 11:28-29. Here is how you may this time using Scripture, say out loud:

"Come to me you who are weary and burdened, and I will give you rest. Take my yoke upon you and learn from me, for I am gentle and humble in heart, and you will find rest for your soul."

Focus on the phrase rest for your soul.

What does that mean for you?

How would that feel?

What is your burden?

Ask Jesus to help you with your burden.

What would it take for you to give him your burden?

*(1),(2),&(3) Sourced in back

"You are still Holy, even when the darkness surrounds my life. Sovereign, you are still sovereign, even when confusion has blinded my eyes." ~Kim Hill; You are Still Holy

"What if the blessings come through rain drops, what if the healing comes through tears, and what if a thousand sleepless nights are what it takes to know your near. And what if trials of this life, are your mercies in disguise."~ Laura Story; Blessings

Chapter 4
Dancing Through Shattered Dreams

I would like to give credit to Dr. Larry Crabb for the comparison I use of Naomi's which is found in the book of Ruth. I read his book "Shattered Dreams"*(1) and absolutely loved it. I have thought of some of the same concepts he used in his book looking at different Biblical characters, however the way Naomi calls out her bitterness and the beauty of the ending that Naomi never saw coming, moved me in such a way that I did not want to sway from also using her story for my book. For further teaching about dancing through shattered dreams, I recommend reading Dr. Larry Crabb's book Shattered Dreams.

There are many different dances we will learn to dance while dancing the dance of life with Christ. We will learn the victory dance, we will learn the dance of hope, and we will learn the authentic love dance. But one dance that is dear to my heart is the dance of shattered dreams. It's a dance I have had to dance on multiple occasions.

Dancing the dance of shattered dreams has many different variations. It may be that there is a loved one fighting the fight for their life. You pray to God with full understanding of His ability to heal and you are full of faith that He will. Only to realize your spouse, child, mother, father, sibling, or best friend will not make it. I've been there more than once. It may sound silly but the time that this particular shattered dream was the worst to dance through was with my beloved dog Rex.

Rex William was a King Shepherd. He was silver sable and he looked just like a wolf. He had been literally removed from his original home due to domestic violence. The husband was abusive to his wife and to Rex. At the time Rex was only a puppy, but he would not be a puppy for long, and King Shepherds are powerful dogs. Everyone could see it was a disaster waiting to happen. Eventually my brother got him, but he had 3 very young girls. Rex was too much energy for tiny little girls. Here enters my family with teenage boys, and of course me an avid animal lover.

We loved Rex. Loved Him! And by the time we got him he loved us too. He had passed through so many people in 8 short months of life, but we gave him the stability he needed, in return he gave us a loyalty that was remarkable. When we went outside in our unfenced acre and a half back yard he would not even think to run off. He would run around but he never took his eye off us (me especially). If I were in the house and my kids were outside and Rex was out with them, Rex would run between the patio door in the house and the garage to make sure he could see all of us.

I even believe Rex was used to save my life. I run at the same time most mornings in the summer. The day I started taking Rex with me to run was the day I noticed a suspicious van parked on the side of the road, running, with no one in it. There was a field on one side, and a forest on the other but no houses where it was parked. After I ran past the van for the second time on my way back to my house, and rounded the corner, the van drove past me. I was suspicious, kept an eye on it, but at first I didn't think much of it. Until I saw it again also secluded the next few times I ran. Of course after the first time I ran with Rex he was my constant running companion. He was a natural and he loved to run with me. If there was any malevolent intent behind the suspicious van, it was deterred by my very large running buddy. I am certain to this day God whispered for me to take Mr. Rex William with me running that first day.

One day I took him with me to do work for a local ministry. A ministry! I didn't want him to be in his cage all day (one area where he wasn't an amazing dog…we could never get him to behave while we were gone.) There was a fenced in area there and sometimes when I went there I would put him in it, or he would just hang out with me in the office and so I took him with me, as I had done several times before.

I had to leave the premises that day for a while, so I put him in the fence. When I returned, the fence door was open, but he was nowhere in sight. I phoned my parents in for reinforcement. We called and called for him. I prayed and begged God to bring him home quickly. We looked for about 10 minutes and I didn't know where else to look, that's when my mom pulled up the long driveway. She yelled, "I found him, he is still alive, but barely. I need your help to get him in the van, hurry!" A car had hit Rex. We think he was looking for me when he got in the road.

To this very day I can still experience that moment as if it were happening right now. He was on the side of the road breathing heavy but not moving. When we picked him up he made a deep, low, moan of pain. There was blood coming out of his mouth. We tried to find a vet near by but it was lunchtime so many offices were closed for the lunch hour. The nearest place that was still open was 20 minutes away, and they were getting ready to go to lunch too. When we called and told them about our situation, they graciously agreed to stay for us. The vet gave us the choice to put him down or to see if he would pull through. He said there was some hope he could survive.

I believed. I knew God could heal him. I prayed Hebrews 11 over him I claimed his healing. I knew Rex would be just fine. I was so angry with my mom and dad's lack of faith when they told me "I think you need to prepare for the worst." How dare they say that to me? Where was their faith? I knew God was about to do a miracle.

You can only imagine my devastation when I called first thing in the morning expecting to hear that during the night Rex had made a full recovery, but instead I heard, "I am so sorry. He died sometime in the night." How could God do that? I was working at a ministry! Doing his work! Why would God give us this wonderful dog and then take him away from us like that? We were supposed to have at least 10 more years with Rex. Did I mention I was working at a ministry… doing work for God?!

To say I struggled with the Rex's death is an understatement. To say I am over it would be a lie. To this day my heart aches and I still have questions. For a long time I was angry with God. I couldn't believe his audacity. Today I think I have a fairly good understanding of why God may have taken away our Rex. One of those reasons has much to do with the fact that I can write about my pain as an example in this book. As a matter of fact, I have used it as a teaching tool in a several instances. I have accepted that God has his reasons and that I don't always understand them. But I still hurt over it.

What about you? Have you experienced a situation similar to this? I know mine is about a beloved pet. Seems silly to some, but others understand that for pet lovers the pet becomes family. Still, I can't help but think if I felt this much anger, grief, and pain over my dog, how much worse it must be for a mother to lose her child. Or a husband to watch helplessly as his wife fades away from cancer; my story was about a dog.

To say God has His reasons seems like a weak answer. There are some situations where there are no good answers and no way to give comfort. How do we dance through those dances with Christ?

Perhaps it is not losing a loved one to death that you are struggling with. Perhaps it is that the relationship itself is dying. You pray with all of your might that God in all of His sovereignty will heal the relationship. And you wait and wait and wait for him to move. But it seems that nothing is happening. He seems silent. Slowly the relationship dies. This may be in the form of a marital relationship, or even a dating relationship. It may be a strained working relationship where you are stuck with that person for better or worse but you can't stand him. Perhaps it is a friendship.

Maybe it's not just the relationship you want saved. Maybe it is their soul. The understanding is that only God can unveil the eyes of the lost. So you cry out to God, "I know you can save this relationship. Only you can speak the truth to my spouse. Unveil his eyes. Call out to his soul. Let him see his need for you. Draw him into you. This marriage is going to end without your divine intervention, Lord, please save it." But in the end he walks away, she cheats, the friendship never finds healing, the lost soul goes to their grave never finding peace with their maker.

Been here too on a few occasions. I knew God was the answer, but I couldn't give that answer to the object of my prayers. God didn't save my first marriage; he didn't swoop in and save other valuable relationships. In some of the circumstances I look back and say "Thank you Jesus for not saving that one. I can't imagine where I would be if you had kept that alive." In other situations I wonder, "Why not God? I can't stop grieving over this loss! Why were you silent?" But God knows what relationships can and should be redeemed and he knows what relationships need to be dead and buried. Sometimes God is working and he is not finished yet, but in our impatient mind he is not going fast enough.

Suppose it is not a life, or relationship that is at the source of your dance of the shattered dreams. Perhaps it is a dream itself. Perhaps you have a vision for a ministry. You pray and pray and pray that God would open doors, or bless this dream you have. But nothing happens. In 2 Samuel 7, King David dreams to build God a temple, but God says, "No, I don't want you to build me a temple. I will build you a kingdom." Letting go of our plans and focusing on God's plans is a tough thing. Sometimes those dreams inside of us ache, but without God's blessing we are dancing our own dance and not following his lead.

Maybe your dream isn't even as noble as a dream of a ministry. Perhaps you just want to go on vacation, or buy new furniture for your home. Maybe you have even lifted this small dream up to God. But every time you begin to save the money something breaks. This may seem like a silly dream to grieve over, especially in light of the types of shattered dreams that we have already talked about. But disappointment is disappointment. It never feels good at any level. Even your little disappoints deserve validation. Besides, little disappointments add up, and can cause a barrier to your inclination to continue in your dance with Christ.

But what does it mean when you dance through shattered dreams? How do we trust in God when all that we hold dear is at stake, and he appears to be withdrawn? I'd like to refer to a story in the Bible to answer that question. It is the story of Naomi and it can be found in the book of Ruth.

A Biblical Example of Dancing in Shattered Dreams

Naomi stared at the graveside of her last son. She had already buried her husband a few years earlier and now both of her children, two sons, were gone as well. There went all of her dreams. When her husband had been alive they had dreams of how their lives would grow and change, as they grew old together. Those dreams died with him. Over the past few years she began to dream again since her boys were now both married. Her dreams consisted of the pitter-patter of little grandbaby feet. But now those dreams were buried well below the ground too. All she had left were her 2 daughters-in-law. They were both so young; they needed to go find new husbands. Naomi knew and understood that soon she wouldn't even have them.

Naomi was in a foreign land. She and her husband came to

Moab 10 years earlier to escape the famine that had hit Bethlehem, her homeland. She had been comfortable in Moab, but her heart always longed to go back to Bethlehem. Now that she had lost everything it made sense to her to find her way back to her roots. She called her daughters-in-law and told them it was time to part ways. They all cried together Orpah kissed Naomi and went back to her family, but Ruth refused to leave her. She told her "Your people will be my people and your God will be my God."

Naomi hesitated. See, she was in a very vulnerable place. A woman in those days did not own property. Her husband did. If she lost her husband, it was up to her sons to care for her and all property went to him. If there were no children she had to find a kinsman redeemer. A kinsman redeemer was a male relative who chose to take responsibility for a relative that was in various types of trouble. One type of trouble is that of a widow with no one else to care for her. If she was young enough he may even give her a child to carry on the dead husband's name and inheritance. But Naomi was too old for more children and things seemed hopeless for her. Naomi was unsure of her own future, to take on the responsibility of Ruth was even more risky. Nonetheless, Naomi agreed to allow Ruth to follow her on the journey, thankful for the companionship, but also worried about both of their wellbeing.

When Naomi and Ruth came up to Naomi's hometown, her old friends came out to greet and welcome her home. "Look," they said, "Isn't this Naomi?"

To which she replied, "Don't call me Naomi, call me Mara. For the Lord has dealt with me bitterly."

See, Naomi means pleasant, Mara means bitter. In this statement Naomi was being bold enough to authentically dance the dance of life through her shattered dreams. She didn't put her crushed feelings or questions up on the shelf and say, "Well, praise God. He's taken my kids and husband from me, but they are in a better place, and he has greater plans." She didn't turn her back on God and run away from him in her anger. She simply accepted her pain, dared to ask the hard questions; all the while she chose to cling to God in the dance.

As we already discussed in chapter 3, God knows our hearts. He created each of us. He knows how our minds work (Psalm 139). He knows we struggle when we have questions and he is fine with that. He doesn't always expect us to move in the dance. He understands it is hard to dance when we are in so much pain we can barely even stand. But he is strong and he can hold us up. In those moments, it's not as much about the dance steps as it is about the embrace. We don't need to have all of the answers and He doesn't always give them to us. But in our struggles, he doesn't always expect us to move; we are sometimes allowed to just sway in his arms.

Long story short, Naomi had a rich kinsman redeemer named Boaz. Boaz fell in love with Ruth. They got married and they had a baby named Obed. The chapter of Ruth ends with Naomi holding Obed, her grandchild. Naomi had danced the dance of shattered dreams, but in it, she found a blessing. She had no idea what would happen when she came back to Bethlehem, but she trusted God to care for her, and he did. God did not give her back the old dreams. She may have still had moments when she missed her husband. She may have still grieved that she would never kiss the cheeks of her sons again. But she delighted in the new dreams God gave her.

Even more important is the story that Naomi never knew on this side of heaven. Obed was the father of Jesse, who was the father of King David, one of the greatest kings to have ever lived. But even bigger is that, King David is in the direct lineage of Jesus Christ, THE KING OF KINGS. Because of Naomi's shattered dreams, and because she chose to dance through those shattered dreams with grace, God orchestrated a story bigger than Naomi could have ever dreamed. Even still, we read about her story thousands of years later. The moment she held that baby on her lap, she could not have known what God would do through her shattered dreams.

Quite honestly, I could have used many different stories in the Bible to talk about dancing through shattered dreams. Joseph had dreams as a child, but God's idea of how it would play out was different than his. I'm sure Joseph never intended to spend years as a slave, and then years in prison for a crime he never committed. King David was confused; I'm sure, as he ran for his life while a maniac tried to kill him. I'm certain David looked back while he was in hiding, to the day that he was anointed and wondered, "What was that day all about? I was sure God had something better planned for me than this, but here I am stuck hiding in caves."

Perhaps my favorite story is how the disciples must have felt as they watched Christ die. He was their hope, and it appeared to be over with Christ's last breath. I try to imagine how they felt as they watched Christ's life fade away, and yet we know that was just the beginning. Over and over again we can see where God used someone's shattered dreams to advance his own glory.

The Created Cannot Understand the Creator

Here is the bottom line though; the created will never understand its creator. The created questions and does not trust. But the creator sees a bigger picture. The day my beautiful baby boys were born, there was no way they could understand me, or this big world they were just born into. They had no idea about the other side of the world, or time, or money. They only knew they had been someplace dark and comfortable, and now they were in a place with lot of sound and commotion and someone that seemed familiar was holding them. I was aware of the bigger picture, but they couldn't understand the picture or me, or anything beyond themselves.

Even as time has passed and my boys are much older and much more sophisticated in their thinking, yet they still can't understand me, their creator. Not long ago I had to change a few things in our home. My 18 & 15-year-old sons began to get angry with me. As they stomped their feet and shook their fists and yelled at me that I did not understand. They told me how wrong it was that I was trying to hold them back. They said I had not poured enough into their lives; I had not done enough for them. They didn't trust me, or my intention for their lives. How dare I…and on and on they went

Once again, the created did not understand the creator. They could not possibly understand what sacrifice was involved when I was 18 years old and found out I was pregnant. In a world where many of my peers chose to end their child's life before it truly began, I chose to give my son life. They could not have understood the sacrifices involved when I was a single mother trying to figure out how to parent two boys. I'm not saying I did it right all the time, in fact I wish I had done much better. I always did my best for where I was in my understanding, but they could not have known all of that.

Throughout their lives I have made many sacrifices and struggled to try to teach them truth in a world as deceitful as ours. I have made so many sacrifices for them that there is no way they could begin to understand, but they sometimes think they do. As they shake their fists and yell at me about how unfair I am, when all I have is their best interest at heart.

If my boys who can see me, and interact with me don't understand me, what makes me think I will ever understand my creator? What makes me think I know what He is doing in my life? But just as I can handle my boys shaking their fists at me, and telling me how unfair I am, God can handle my questions, anger, and fear. But the question he ultimately has is "Will you dance with me through this?" Trust me, rest in my arms.

Even as I write this, God is asking me to dance with him through my shattered dreams. We have been dancing through these shattered dreams for years now. I have hurts that will not heal, I have questions that he will not answer, or he answers with "The answer will come at an appointed time, and this is not it. Wait." It hurts, and it is hard. I wish I had great testimony that said I conquered the dance of shattered dreams. I am now a master. But I'm not. I can tell you this though:

When Christ asked me to dance the dance of life, it was engulfed in dancing through shattered dreams. I had to leave some things behind that I did not want to leave. It was hard. It hurt. Some of those things still hurt, but I can tell you now I can see his reasons.

There was a time that life ripped the rug out from under me. I remember laying on the floor in deep despair; I questioned that day if I even wanted to continue my dance with Christ. I blamed him in part for the situation I was in. Looking back now I can see it was all about the embrace in that moment. I can also see it was a moment where my character was refined and I was strengthened.

Early on in my dance with Christ, I was learning about tithing and trust. There were several moments I prayed , "After paying the bills there is only $50 in the checkbook. God, if I tithe I will only have $10 and we do not have groceries. Do you still expect me to tithe?" I cannot tell you how hard it was to give to God in those moments. The songs we sing in church about "…blessed be your name in the land marked with suffering though there is pain in the offering blessed be your name…" Is so different when you are truly facing starving for a week. But do you know that God provided in every instance. One way or another money that I did not expect showed up.

Dancing the dance of shattered dreams is one of the hardest dances to dance. But there is beauty in it too. God has a way of holding your heart in a way that no one else can, but only if you allow him to; only if you are willing to sit in the pain and disappointment of your shattered dreams. We live in a society that runs from disappointment. We medicate our pain either by numbing out in distraction, cheap relationships, or illicit and prescription drugs, or alcohol. When we run, we miss out on the beauty of refinement and growth. We also miss the opportunity to heal.

Dancing the dance of shattered dreams runs the risk of never fully healing. Carolyn James*(2) points out "In a real sense, he (Job) would always be a sufferer. It is important for us to see this because so many of our own struggles have pain in the epilogue—there isn't a near resolution and our fortunes don't take an upward turn. But God's plan isn't defined by happy endings; neither is it about getting answers to all of our questions."

God has his reasons. Many of his reasons will remain a mystery. Some of his reasons we will know, like my story about Rex. As I said earlier, I have used him as an object lesson in so many different ways; God and his loving boundaries, how God gives us more freedom when we don't want to chase unhealthy things, love for our master, and of course I have now written about it in this book. In this case I have a full answer for my grief, yet the grief will always remain.

There are other pains I have no answers for, I probably never will. My faith must stay in my understanding that God is always faithful. He knows what is best for not only me, but also all of those around me. How many times has my life been changed for the better when I hear stories of people who have suffered great atrocities, and yet clung to their faith in God? Sometimes God allows things to happen because he knows that our witness to others, some who we will never even meet, will be life changing for them. Sometimes the way we handle our pain will benefit his kingdom. We must remember this and make a conscious effort to hold firm to these truths while we are dancing the dance of shattered dreams.

*(1)&(2) sourced in back

"The places I long for the most, are the places where I've been they keep calling out to me like a long lost friend."
~Sarah Groves, Painting Pictures of Egypt

"Be Solitary, Be Silent, and Be At Peace."~ Unknown

"This is my prayer in the desert; When all that's within me feels dry this is my prayer my hunger and my need. My God is the God who provides"~ Hill Song; Desert Song

Chapter 5
Dancing Through the Desert

We have all heard the story about How God freed the Israelites, but let's look at it again, perhaps in a new way. Israel had spent hundreds of years in bondage to the Egyptians. Throughout the years they cried out to God for freedom. Finally, after generations of prayers God showed up. God showed himself not only to the Israelites but also to the Egyptians through plagues that were specifically sent to mock the false gods of Egypt. Pharaoh did not want to release God's people, but after God's final plague where he took Pharaoh's first-born son, he relinquished. Initially the Israelites began praising God, they were energized and encouraged as they started off on their journey of freedom. But only three days later their tune changed, as the ambiguity of their journey began to set in.

Once they entered the desert of Shure the journey became tough. They were hot, tired, thirsty and uncomfortable. God had not provided for them the way they expected him to and they were getting frustrated with him. As the weeks went by they began to long for the familiarity of "home". They craved the meat pots they got in Egypt. Sure, back in Egypt they were slaves, in bondage to the Egyptians, but the discomfort of the slavery began to fade. The memories of the good things in their lives while in Egypt began to illuminate. They were yet to taste the beauty of their promised land; at this point the land was little more than an intangible dream or an idea. What if there were no meat pots in the Promised Land? What if they never even made it to the Promised Land? Or worse yet, what if God was lying and there was no promised land? Maybe they never should have left their "comfortable" homes in Egypt, the place of their bondage.

    As the time in the desert went on, they began to grow discontented and they began to complain against Moses and God. When Moses went up to Mount Sinai to fellowship with God, he didn't come back when they expected him to. The people became restless. They were unsure of what had happened to Moses. Maybe he abandoned them, or perhaps he died. Questions of "What if he never comes back" began to plague them. Fear that they would all die in the desert waiting around for Moses began to infiltrate the camp. They decided they needed to do something to help things along. Perhaps it was time to bring other gods, the gods from their days in bondage, into the situation. And so, each family donated gold to create a golden calf to bow down and worship. Since Yaweigh, God was taking too long to do what they wanted him to do; they would find another god to do it.

    I'm so glad that we don't ever behave like the Israelites…or do we? I know that I can look back on times where God had released me from some form of bondage I had put myself in. At first I felt free and excited, but as time went on I would yearn for some of the good that I had while I was in slavery. Let's face it, we don't put ourselves in bondages that are void of fun, they start out a place of refuge. But before we know it we are slaves. Just as the Israelites were, I have been guilty thinking that when God releases me from my slavery that I should step immediately into blessing. When it didn't happen that way I became frustrated and angry with him. God does not usually work that way, if it ever happens like that, I can assure you it is very rare. Waiting is not fun, but there is a refinement that happens in the journey of the desert.

    There are two specific things I'd like to focus on in this chapter;

the first thing is the desert itself. As we will discuss our deserts may look very much like the above story of the Israelites, or it may be very different. Either way the desert is a place that is uncomfortable. The other thing I would like to focus on is the idols we are prone to bow to in the desert. As we will see later, sometimes we try to take our idols into the Promised Land with us.

The Israelites time in the desert followed a period of a great movement of God's power. For weeks God had plagued the Egyptians, then he parted the sea to allow them to pass, and suddenly there was silence. God appeared to withdraw his presence from the Israelites. Have you been here? Me too. Times in my life where it is painful and God is silent, or tragedy strikes and I have no sense of direction and God feels distant. Or a time when nothing is moving, I am at a complete standstill. I pray and beg and plead with God, but nothing happens; just silence. All of these are characteristics of the desert; dry, weary, silent, stifling, and painful.

The Three Types of Desert

Sometimes the desert feels like God is punishing you, but there is always a purpose for it. In Scriptures I can find numerous examples of the desert. There is the desert where the Israelites are between their bondage, and the promise land. It was kicked off by a time of God's very profound presence but it was followed by dryness, ambiguity, and discomfort. The Israelites got into trouble for grumbling complaining and their doubt. You may feel a little confused here because earlier in the book I mentioned how it is good to be genuine with your feelings. Speak your disappointments and true feelings. But now I am saying it was wrong for the Israelites to complain. It may seem contradictory. Let me see if I can clarify.

Desert Number One

In the book Leaving Egypt authored by Chuck DeGroat*(1), he explains that complaining is expressing the emotion with a lack of faith and an intention to turn back to the bondage. You can see this is what the Israelites were doing, and God was fed up with them. When we are in the desert, we are free to cry out, and express our genuine feelings, but we must not turn back to our bondage. There are times when I freely express my anger and confusion at God, but follow it up immediately with a confession that I recognize I am sinful and God is God. I confess that I recognize my own human frailties, and God sees and knows all. This is a healthy way to deal with feelings. At these moments we need to beg God to step into the turmoil.

Desert Number Two

Another purpose for the desert may be for preparation. I see this not only in the book of Samuel where David is wandering in the wilderness for years before he enters his kingship, but it is also seen with Jesus just before he enters his ministry. In both cases it is clear that the desert/wilderness is specifically for preparation.

In the case of David, he was anointed as future king over Israel when he was still a young boy. At the time David may not have realized that the anointing was setting him apart to be king, however he would have recognize that he was being set apart by God for some reason. I can only imagine how confused he was immediately after his anointing when life went back to normal. Shortly after the anointing, the hand of God did indeed move, but not in the way expected. David made a connection with Saul the current king over Israel. Initially Saul liked David, but soon he was running for his life from Saul. During this time David found himself in the desert, hiding in caves. As we read the Psalms we can hear David's despair during this time in his life.

As we read the story, we can see how God used the desert for David to build his character. During his time in the desert he learned to trust in God, and to listen for God's direction. He also learned lessons in leadership as he led a large group of men while in the desert. God allowed David's desert, and though it was not comfortable and it was hard, it had a purpose for refinement in David's character. His time in the desert was meant to prepare him for leading the great nation of Israel. We can glean a lot of wisdom from David's story during the years of the desert. He went through many different emotions, he had several questions, but he always stood firm on his faith in God's character.

We see another example of the desert or wilderness for preparation in the life of Jesus. When he was baptized a dove descended upon him for all to see. Then God called from the heavens "This is my beloved Son" and all who stood near by heard the proclamation. Instead of this declaration catapulting him into greatness, we next see Jesus going onto the wilderness for 40 days. For Jesus, the wilderness was his desert. Just like David before him, Jesus was being prepared for his ministry.

During his preparation Satan took the opportunity to tempt Jesus. I used to believe that Jesus' temptation was at the very end of his time in the wilderness and it was not that hard on him. Just a few quick sentences spoken between Jesus and Satan and then it was over. I no longer believe that. I have been tempted. I now know that temptation can be oppressive, and it can feel almost like torture. It takes great strength to stand firm.

Some people say simply speak against the temptation, I have tried this, but it does not always lift the oppression. Jesus himself faced an oppressive kind of temptation; yet he stood firm through it. Hebrews 2:18 says he suffered when he was tempted. Be sure that when temptation is painful, God is doing a work in you, but also be sure he understands how painful some temptations can be.

Desert Number Three

The final type of desert I find in Scripture is when Elijah runs for his life from Jezebel. He runs into the desert and asks God to take his life. God uses this time as a time of resting and restoration for him. Elijah was receptive of it, but in our culture many of us do not do the desert of any kind well, perhaps least of all the desert of rest and restoration. We don't like to rest, somehow we think that busyness is evidence of productivity, and too much rest is evidence of laziness. Never mind that most of our busyness is little more than running in circles, at least we feel important. But God sees it necessary for times to rest in the desert. It is time for Christians to learn to rest when God leads us to the desert for restorative purposes. Again, I am not one who has this mastered; I have a hard time with the desert of rest. When God leads me away to rest, I will quickly dive into training for a race of some sort, or studying up on some sort of ministry I would love to start, or I can even be guilty of running around all day but accomplishing absolutely nothing. When God leads us into an Elijah moment it is important to be receptive of it.

Fashioning false gods

I have given examples of the desert in Biblical terms, but of course you know in today's society the desert looks very different. I have been through many dry spells, and I believe I may have many more to endure. It is while we are in the desert we begin to feel drawn to bow to idols, or look to something other than God for comfort or relief. Sometimes those idols are obviously wrong, such as pornography, drugs or alcohol, but some idols are much more subtle.

Years ago, I was called to go back to college. I did not have a degree at the time, just a couple classes under my belt. I knew I was called to school and God anointed me for the task, much like David before his desert experience. When I graduated from college I WAS READY!!!! I was ready to be used by God. I was full of ideas and dreams. I had proposals written up for ministries I wanted to start, but nothing came of it. I started one ministry that God clearly shut down. I finally got the idea I was to wait, and wait I still am doing, but it took a good year and a half before I learned to wait quietly. This desert has given me more than one lesson in humility, steadfastness, patience, and trust.

Today, the sermon at church was about finding your purpose and beginning to live it. My heart grieved a bit and even felt a little bitter because I am an individual on the other side of the pastor's urging. I don't need to be encouraged to do something for Christ. I have an idea of my purpose, I have prayed and studied and I want to do it, but God has said "not yet". And so here I wait in the desert. It is tempting to create some idols of self-importance, or ministry that has not been ordained by God. In fact, I have used my dreams as a source of security, and looked to my talents for answers. To be boldly honest, I have used them as my idols. It was my security for a while, not God. Isn't that what the Israelites did? God wasn't working out the way they wanted, so they fashioned a golden calf to come be their new security instead of waiting on him.

 Right now I am in a desert for preparation. Much like David it is a long desert, and it is hard. My life is not threatened, I have a place to lay my head, but I am fighting to hold tight to God's character of goodness, even as it feels there is little good to see. I have bowed to my idols of comfort; I have clung to my gifts and talents for security. But God sits on his throne and only he can lead me into the victory of whatever lies ahead for me. As the years tick by I am learning to stop clinging to false securities, and cling to God's character instead.

 The desert after bondage is a little different than my current desert, but I have been there too. Have you ever prayed and prayed for freedom from some form of bondage? Only to long for "the good old days" once you have been released. I know of a lady who has been addicted to heroine. She once said that everyday is a struggle to stay sober. She has been released from the slavery of her addiction, she no longer does what her former "master" tells her to, but she craves the high everyday, even though satisfying her longing for the high kept her in slavery. It is the time between our release from bondage and our arrival to the Promised Land that we are most vulnerable to falling down in worship of our idols.

 What we may not realize is though it brings some form of relief; our idols are still a form of bondage. The Israelites made an idol they were familiar with while in slavery. Apis and Hathor were both the Egyptian gods that had the form of a cow. They made an idol out of something familiar and comfortable to them when God seemed silent. We are all in slavery at some point in our lives. Some of mine were, my own spontaneous passions, romance, alcohol, and my selfish desires. We all have those kinds of idols. While in bondage I became familiar with some gods that were not really God. After I was freed from bondage I did indeed bring some idols with me for the journey. An idol is anything that takes precedence over God, or even family. We all have a throne in our heart, what sits on that throne? Is it God? Do you try to let God share your throne with other things? Be careful when you answer this, some idols can be good except for the status they hold in your life and some are not as prevalent as others.

Seeking Out Hidden Idols

As we grow in our relationship with Christ, the idols become less obvious. When I was newly out of slavery, my idols were obvious. There were times I desperately wanted to turn to some of them yet, I stood firm and felt satisfaction when I was strong enough to resist them. As time has gone by, some of those idols have lost the hold they once had on me. I am still passionate, but my passions are controlled and more focused on doing God's work and not on getting into trouble. I still long for romance, but I am not controlled by a desperate need for it. Some Christians believe it is o.k. To drink some do not. I am not addressing that in this book, but I feel each Christian needs to weigh it out for themselves. For myself, it can be an idol. It is easy for me to fall down and indulge in it when I felt the discomfort of the desert. I am very careful about drinking; I want to wait on God to bring me my relief rather than alcohol.

Those are all obvious idols, but recently, I have begun to seek out those deeper idols. Those that are not as easy to recognize. These are what I am calling my "vices". Or I may even call them my false props. When I changed the question from "what are my idols" to "What are my vices", my answer changed dramatically. See, I don't see coffee as an idol, but I do see myself dependent on it. I don't see a latte' from Starbucks as some form of evil, but I do see an unhealthy relationship with it when I think I need a large one everyday at $5 per cup. I see a problem with it when I am scrimping around for change to try to find the money for at least a tall latte' (smallest size). This may be a flag that there is a form of dependency upon it. I am looking to it for some sort of relief. This is exactly what an idol is.

In 1 Corinthians 6:12 Paul says, "I will not be mastered by anything." I have masters. I am mastered by my love for pizza, gum, coffee, Starbucks and a couple other things. I know you may be saying, "Oh come on Michele, you cannot seriously think it is a sin to drink coffee." Absolutely not! I don't, nor do I intend to give it up for good, however I now have an awareness of those little vices in my life. Those things that keep me spoiled. The things I indulge in. I don't want them to have power over me, therefore I have deemed them my idols and I have determined that they will not master me.

Looking for those deep idols, the ones that on the surface may not be sinful yet still have an unhealthy hold on you, can be a form of worship and a way to grow in your relationship with Christ. While writing this chapter I decided I wanted to give up coffee for a time. I didn't decide to give it up because I thought I might go to hell if I didn't, I didn't give it up as a fasting prayer thing, I gave it up, as a simple sacrifice, something that I hoped would put a smile on God's face. I don't include this information in my book to brag, someone once said, "The moment you tell others about a sacrifice you make for God, you lose the blessing." I hope I don't, but if I do, that's ok. My hopes in telling you about this form of self-denial is not for my own glory, but so you may look to your own idols, prayerfully consider giving them up for a time and grow a little deeper in your own relationship with Christ.

I would like to clarify that physical things are not the only idols we have. I have been guilty of using my status as an idol, or my talents, or my ministry. I bow down to what God will do through me and for me in the name of Jesus. But it is my heart full of pride and it is the gifting that I worship, not God.

I am a singer. I love to sing and I know that God has used my song to bless the hearts of many. Truly, when I sing, I am singing only to God and it is from my heart. But there has been jealousy in my heart toward others who sing. There was also a time when I thought the only gift I could offer God was my singing. Though my heart truly worshiped God in my song, my song was my idol. God actually had to strip me of my ministry through song in order for me to get this idol where it was meant to be. Even today the ministry I once was given has never been restored, but I have peace about that. I may never sing as much as I once did, but I have so much more to give God than my song. I am no longer aching to sing. That gift has lost its hold over me.

These are examples of hidden idols I have bowed to while in my deserts. Even coffee I have noticed is something I long for while in a desert. The other day I was having a real bad day; the yearning for coffee grew even stronger on that day. It is a vice that I have even in my good moments, but I recognize now the desire to look to it for comfort gets stronger in my desert.

Bringing Idols Into the Promised Land

It is a great dream to believe that once in the Promised Land the Israelites saw that God is good and they were able to follow the second commandment "You shall not make idols", but it was not so. I can see this in several places in Scripture but in the book of Judges alone, I can see 2 circumstances where idols were set up in the name of Jehovah God.

The first is in Judges 8. For years I had heard the story of Gideon, the great warrior of God who went up against the Midianites. It was not until I recently looked a little closer at this story that I realized how much idol worship was a part of this story.

Israel began to do evil in the eyes of the Lord by worshipping like the Amorites, in whose land they were sharing. The displeasing worship included idol worship. As a result of breaking the second commandment, God allowed Israel to fall into oppression under the Midianite Army.

I want to stop there for a moment to give you a moment to reflect on the significance of this. There were harsh consequences to Israel breaking God's law in this story. God handed them over to bondage and persecution, simply because they gave themselves permission to do things their way not God's. There are times in my life that I know what is the right thing to do, yet I choose to give myself permission to indulge in what I want anyway. If God gave consequences of oppression to Israel his chosen nation, won't he do the same to us who are also his chosen people? Hebrews 12:6 says God disciplines those that he loves. He disciplined Israel because he loved them, he will discipline the rest of us because he loves us too.

Israel cries out to God, yet they continue in their sin. God sends a prophet as a response, yet even as the prophet explains the oppression is a consequence to their sin, Israel continues to bow down to things that are not God. Finally, the Angel of God comes to give Gideon a commission. The first thing Gideon is told to do is cut down his father's idol and alter to Baal and then build a proper alter for God, followed by a proper sacrifice to God on the new alter.

It is clear that God will not free Israel until idols are cleared out, and proper recognition and worship are given to him. I want to pause here for a moment again. Where in your life have you asked for victory, yet God is not moving? Are there idols, even hidden ones there? If so it may be time to cut down those idols and build an appropriate alter for God and find some appropriate sacrifices. Obedience is always part of the dance with Christ.

From here I want to fast forward to the end. So many things happen between clearing of the idols, and Gideon's victory. It's a great story and if you have not read it yet I recommend you read it for yourself in Judges 6-8. If you have read it, it may be great to go back and read it again. But the end is what shocked me. After all the problems with idols in this story, after all of the victory after clearing out the idols Gideon collects gold from their enemy, and makes an ephod. The last few words before the telling of Gideon's death says this, "All Israel prostrated themselves by worshiping it (the ephod) there, and it became a snare to Gideon and his family." Judges 8:27 NIV.

An ephod was a garment of clothing that the high priest would wear. Some resources say that the ephod itself was likely on a golden image fashioned by man. I believe that Gideon did this thinking it was to "honor" God, since an ephod was used in connection with Jehovah God. But it was not honoring at all, it was still idol worship and it became a snare to Gideon.

Are you as baffled as I am? What in the world was he thinking?? They were just released from oppression because of idol worship, and the very first thing they do is start worshiping an ephod; yes ephods are connected to God, but they are not God.

I believe we do the same thing in our culture. We get set free and we begin to worship the experience of getting set free. Some people worship the idol of finding their breakthrough moment, or an emotional experience from God. I have been to church events where no one is allowed to leave until there is emotional movement "by the spirit". When the "experience of God" is the focus, and not God himself we are caught up in idol worship.

As I mentioned before when it is our status, our gifting, our talents, our ministry that is the focus we have lost sight of the one true God, and we are guilty of falling down to worship idols in Jesus' name. Again, I have to confess I am guilty. I do not teach because I have anything mastered, I teach because I am learning from my own flaws. You have my permission to be flawed as well, but you never have permission to wallow in the flaws. Falling into idol worship out of ignorance is one thing, but it is wrong to stay in ignorance. God does not honor self-indulgence to our idols, he is a jealous God, and for good reason. None of my idols ever gave up a child for me, suffered for me, and died for me. None of my idols have healed me or given me life.

Only God deserves all of my honor and praise.

A final thought is that we can be guilty of idol worship when we fashion God in our perceived image of who we want him to be. God is the God he is. We don't make him, he made us, yet we try to make him behave the way we want him to. Some people in our culture turn God into an all loving, non punishing God who would never send anyone to hell. Though it is true he is an all-loving God, it is not true that he will not hold people accountable for their life long rebellious spirit to God. Other's want to turn God into a magic genie, or an angry God. When we begin to put God into our own boxes, we are guilty of fashioning a false god.

Dancing through the desert is a tricky task. It is even more tricky to dance in the desert and cling to the one true God without switching partners whether it be intentionally by bowing to the idols of our days in bondage or beginning to dance with a counterfeit version of god. But that is not an excuse to dance carelessly. Dancing in the desert is a time to dance with intention and determination. Even in his silence Christ will never let us go, which is all the more reason to not lose sight of the promise and let go of him.

*(1) Sourced in back

"Stand in the rain, stand your ground stand up when it's all crashing down. You stand through the pain, you won't drown and one day, what's lost can be found. You stand in the rain." ~Superchick

"Be still my soul, be still. Be still my soul be still. Wait patiently upon the Lord and be still my soul be still." ~Kari Jobe

Chapter 6
Dancing in the Storm

I remember years ago standing in the living room of an elderly man who had just lost his wife to whom he had been married to for well over 50 years. We were discussing marriage and how it was tough to stay together and work things out. I asked him in a world full of divorce what made the difference, he replied "Hurricanes whip through the land with wind speeds over 150 miles an hour, when it is over one thing remains standing and that is the palm tree because it has learned to bend a little." Throughout marriage, couples will face multiple storms, but isn't this advice true for all storms in life?

It may be a sand storm that takes place in the desert, it may be a storm of glass in our shattered dreams, it may be a thunderstorm, blizzard, or hurricane, but we all have storms in life, and each one looks very different. There are many reasons for those storms. Some storms are thrown on us because of someone else's choices. Sometimes God allows storms to come to test us, grow us, or other reasons that we may not understand. Two times in Scripture we see where Satan asks for permission to bring a storm into someone's life (Job, Luke 22:31). And then there are the storms we bring on ourselves. I may be wrong, but I believe the last one named is the worst because they are preventable storms, and yet we are the ones responsible for bringing the pain on ourselves. No matter what the reason is for the storm, God can use them as a way to refine us. The biggest key to surviving all storms without losing our sanity is to cling to God's truth.

What does Scripture say about dancing through the storms?

> *"God is our refuge and strength*
> *an ever-present help in trouble*
> *Therefore we will not fear, though the earth gives way*
> *And the mountains fall into the heart of the sea*
> *Though the waters foam and the mountains quake with their surging…*
> *…Be still and know that I am God." Psalm 46*

We are to be still, yet it is human nature to want to take action when we are faced with a difficult time. When we feel loss, we want to grasp at anything to regain control, when we feel broken we feel an urge to fix it. Being still and waiting does not feel like an option, yet this is exactly what we are called to do.

Remember in the chapter about shattered dreams when I said sometimes it is not as much about the dance steps as it is about the embrace? Sometimes during the storms of life we are simply called to wait them out. Hunker down and take it quietly, let Jesus hold you in the wind, and torrent. When the violent downpour lets up for a moment, begin to dance in the rain until the next one let's loose.

Waiting hurts. We don't do it well. In a world full of microwave dinners, fast food restaurants, on demand TV, and high speed Internet, we are used to getting what we want when we want it. No waiting. If the internet doesn't bring up the page we Google searched within .5 seconds we hit the search button 5 more times to try to hurry it along. If the line at Starbucks is really long we tap our foot and sway back and forth until it is our turn, we grow restless at the stoplights, uncertain what to do until it turns green again. If we get this uncomfortable waiting in everyday life how much worse are we when we are dancing through a painful, anxiety filled storm as we wait for Christ to show up and give us some relief? It is especially hard when we have no idea how long our wait may be.

The other day I was reading something on Facebook about funny things women in labor say. One woman decided that she was done halfway through the labor pains. She didn't want to do it anymore. She actually got up and tried to go home. The problem of course is that she was in labor. The only way she will be done with it is when it is over. She can try to take matters into her own hands and go home, but that will not make the pain go away. We laugh at this, but how many times have I been in the midst of a storm and decided I was done. I ruminate, and grasp for answers and attempt some actions, but none of it relieves the discomfort of my storm. In fact, sometimes that makes it worse.

So what are we to do? I like what Rick Warren says*(1). In his blog… he talks about the time Paul was caught up in the storm, and became shipwrecked. The crew was unable to see the sun or stars for days, they lost their compass, and so they drifted. They threw things overboard that they needed, cargo and supplies. They were trying to do something to help the situation, of course all they did was throw over board all of their food, supplies and belongings. Paul on the other hand never lost his compass. God had promised him they would all survive so he stood firm on God's promises.

Just as Paul did, we must learn to be still, and keep our focus on God. We need to be deliberate not to throw precious things like our dreams or moral values over board during our storms in life. Desperate situations sometimes lead to desperate choices, but not if we learn to stand firm in truth. One of the best ways to do this is to first be deliberate in quieting your mind before the Lord. Learn to sit, quiet in silence, patiently before the Lord. Maybe start with 1 minute a day. Shut down all worry, all agendas. Rest for just a moment in the presence of God. Add to the time as you learn to be still before the

Lord. It is hard, especially since our culture in constantly restless. But when you learn to quiet yourself, you will find peace and relief. Next, dig into the Scriptures for strength. Here are a few Scriptures that speak directly to waiting out the storms of life:

Lamentations 3:25-26 The Lord is good to those who hope in him, it is good to wait quietly on his salvation

Psalm27: 13-14 Be confident in God's goodness, be strong and wait

Psalm 37:7 Be still before the Lord, do not fret when evil seems to succeed.

Psalm 62:5 Find rest in the Lord, my hope is in Him

Psalm 130:5 My soul waits for the Lord, I put my faith in His word

Psalm 112:He that is steadfast in his trust will have no fear

James 5:7-8 Be patient for the Lord's coming, just as the farmer waits for his crops. Stand firm as you wait

1 Corinthians 15:58 Stand firm, do not let anything move you

Hebrews 6:18 Be encouraged, it is impossible for God to lie

Hebrews 6:19 Let the hope God offers you be your anchor for the soul

And perhaps my personal favorite:

> *Habakkuk 2:3 "The revelation awaits an appointed time. It speaks of the end. It will not prove false. Though it linger, wait for it; it will certainly come and not delay."*

This is my favorite because it is important. Answers will come, God will move. All will be known at an appointed time, though it linger it will come. However, if we don't wait, the revelation may take a lot longer. Or we may cause the journey to the goodness God has for us to become a longer journey. He can redeem our mistakes, but isn't it better to be still, trust in God's goodness, and wait for His first plan of goodness? I have messed up his plans by rushing to find answers that weren't mine to get yet. Though it linger wait, it will come when it is meant to. Wait out the storm.

Dancing in the storms is about learning how to quiet your mind. It is a discipline. It is about learning to sit in the pain, fear, or discomfort. It is learning to not rush ahead of God in the dance steps, but learning when and how to move, following his lead in the dance. It is about trusting God even when the torrent of rain is so blinding, the thunder deafening, when the lightning is so close the hair on your arms stand on end. It is about resting, stillness. Not rushing to move, not trying to dance away from the storm, giving up the need to be in control or fix, and simply learning to rest.

When we learn to do this, Christ has the opportunity to show us that he can and will come through. He is faithful to us when we put our faith in him. I know this to be true, and yet even as I type this last sentence, I am once again being tested as to whether or not I believe my own words here. But I cling to the knowledge that God has come through for me in the past, and one way or another he will again.

*(1) Sourced in back

"I wanna live for you, I wanna die to me. I want to be empty I want to be free from all that holds me captive all that brings me down all that's tried to lose me now that I've been found. I want to live for you." ~ Live for You, Connorsvine

"I know it's gonna kill me but I just can't let it go. And the taste so appealing it's got a grip unpon my soul. These honey dipped lies mesmerize me.~Lecrae; Killa

"I'd rather fight You for what I don't really want than to take what you give that I need" ~Hold Me Jesus, Big Daddy Weave

Chapter 7
Dead Man Dancing

Can I be completely honest with you and still maintain some level of your respect? I am among those people who believe in the zombie apocalypse. In fact, I don't just believe in it, I know it to be real. To be clear, there is a slight difference between the zombies I am talking about and the ones you would traditionally think of. The zombies I know to be real are not ugly, rotted carcasses walking around trying to kill people. Real zombies are beautiful, alluring, and almost irresistible. I suppose they look more like today's version of vampires; they draw you in with their beauty and charm. They are not out to kill you in a violent death, they want to appeal to you and kill your spiritual life in a slow, self-gratifying manor.

Galatians 5:24 states that if we belong to Christ we have crucified the flesh. In Matthew, Mark, and Luke Jesus is quoted saying that if we wish to follow Jesus we must pick up our cross daily to follow him, and Ephesians 4:22 says we must put off the old self which is corrupt. Also in Matthew and in Luke we find several references to how those who lose their lives for Christ's sake will find life (Matthew 10:39; 16:25; 6:25 and Luke 17:33).

We are all born with a sinful nature. The concept was already discussed all the way at the beginning of this book. We were made for unity with God, but our sinful nature wanted control and that unity was broken. We are naturally born sinners. Have you ever met a 2 year old who needed to learn to tell his parents "no"? Or have you met a three year old who had to be taught not to share? Has anyone ever had to teach a 6 year old to lie to stay out of trouble? Of course not! We do those things by nature.

Galatians 5:19 says the acts of the sinful desire are obvious: sexual immorality, impurity, debauchery, idolatry, witchcraft, hatred, discord, jealousy, fits of rage, selfish ambition, dissensions, factions, envy, drunkenness, orgies and the like. I don't know about you but I have been guilty of at minimum desiring many of these things, and no one had to tempt me into actually doing some of them. I wanted to indulge. Fits of rage can be satisfying in the moment. Dissension with someone I don't like is very gratifying, especially when I win (and I can be good at winning).

But when we accept Christ we are new creations (2 Cor. 5:17). The old self has been shed and we are new in Christ. The problem is that old self still somewhat influences us. Our old self may die, but he resurrects…a lot. This old self is the flesh or the natural self. The old self dies, the new creation is formed but the old self appears as a stubborn zombie who refuses to give up what he wants. When he resurrects he is beautiful. My old self knows exactly what words to speak to me to get my attention, she can appeal to my most vulnerable places. She reminds me of my rights when someone has spoken harshly to me, though the new self is called to be patient and kind to them. The zombie will remind me of how much I deserve to be recognized at work for all that I have done, even though I am called to be humble in spirit and work for my boss submissively as though working for my heavenly Father.

The old self will remind you how much you deserve to indulge in too much wine Friday night because it was a rough week. Or how relaxing it would be to read a novel and 50 Shades of Grey has peaked your interest. The old self will remind you that your wife has not been intimate with you in weeks, and it is late, no one is up, and the lustful gratification is only the click of a button away. The old self will rise, and he knows how to appeal to your senses, your pride, and your deepest desires, because the old self is still a part of you. This is not a crucifixion that takes place once. But it must happen daily, or sometimes several times a day.

I literally take moments at times to envision myself dragging my old self, to the alter of my heart, strapping her down, taking my knife, stabbing it into her over and over again, and then burning her on that alter as a sacrifice to God. But just as I have turned my back and begun to walk away she is alive and right behind me again, whispering to me about my rights and my needs. If I am to follow Christ, I am to lose my life. Forget my desires, ignore my flesh, pick up my cross daily and follow Jesus.

The death is painful. It hurts. It must be intentional.

In the book the Seeking Heart author Fenlon*(1) says of dying to self, "Your Father wastes no time cutting onto that which is already dead. If he wanted to let you remain as you are he would certainly do so. He seeks to destroy your old nature. He can only do this by cutting into what is alive."

"Many think that dying to themselves is what causes them so much pain. But it is actually part of them that still lives that causes the problem."

How Does Crucifying Flesh Connect to Previous Chapters?

Crucifying the flesh is the key element to a successful dance in the chapters about the genuine dance, dancing through shattered dreams, dancing through the desert, and dancing through the storms.

See, during those tough times we may want to react in ways that are contrary to the nature of Christ. These are some of the most vulnerable times for us to fall victim to the attack of the zombie apocalypse.

When dancing through genuineness we may be tempted to act on some of the desires we are pulling off the shelf and facing for the first time, or we may be tempted to walk away from Christ because we are finally feeling the depth of our anger toward him. We may be tempted to keep genuine feelings neatly hidden on the shelf, or tempted to continue in our false piety. All are acts of our flesh.

While dancing through shattered dreams we may be tempted to put our genuine feelings on the shelf, or hide from the pain and disappointment. We may indulge in numbing techniques, or we may not want to stand firm through the tough times. We may reject the truth that encourages us to hold firm to Jesus. We may allow the darkness to completely overtake us. These are also acts of our flesh.

During our time of Dancing in the desert, we may choose to ignore the fact that there are areas of false support that we have set up around us. We may ignore the fact that we are daily bowing down to idols, or we may justify our behavior. We may refuse to sit in the discomfort of the desert and wait on God. These are still acts of the flesh.

The flesh does what is comfortable in the moment, with no thought to what future consequences are. The flesh does not think about it's behavior and how it interferes with a relationship with God's Spirit. Ephesians 4:30 says, "Do not grieve the spirit of God. Do not quench the spirit." Anything that comes from self-love, from the flesh, grieves God's spirit. The Person controlled by the spirit does not indulge in the temptation that the walking dead man whispers to him. He controls his urges. He drags the zombie to the alter of his heart, ties him down, and does his best to destroy it. Doing so takes strength that is not found in one's self, it requires taking your vulnerabilities to God and asking him for strength. I have actually felt God offer me his strength as I dance through this dance. There were times I was so weak that he offered strength to me breath by breath. Every time God offered me his strength, I had to choose to grab hold of the faith, to keep going. But I could have chosen to reject his strength and fall to my weakness.

On the other hand, the person controlled by the flesh will indulge and then justify himself for doing so. Again, I feel compelled to confess to you, I don't have this art mastered. I have my weaknesses. And though that list of weaknesses keep shrinking as God sanctifies me, there are still a few things that I continue to indulge in and justify.

How Do I Identify What pleases the Flesh?

One sure way to know if you are pleasing the flesh, and not God's Spirit is to ask yourself if there is any shame in your behavior. Would you do this behavior if someone else were watching? What if it were a member at your church? What if it were the pastor in the church? What if Jesus himself walked in and saw you doing that behavior, or heard your thoughts? If there is any shame connected to your behavior then stop, it's likely grieving God's Spirit. I have told my kid's on numerous occasions, "If you don't want me to telling your grandparents or my friends about what you did, then maybe you shouldn't be doing it." If you feel like you have to cover it up, don't do it.

Another way is to stop justifying yourself and listen to what your hearts pull is telling you. There was a behavior I felt like God wanted me to quite, but it is somewhat acceptable in some Christian circles, and not so much in others. I was reluctant to give it up. I did not feel ashamed of this act, not in itself, but I felt as though God wanted me to give it up for him. There was a pull there for years that I justified, but when I finally submitted to what my hearts pull was telling me, there was immediate blessing and relief.

Both of the above has to do with acting in good conscience. Acts 24:16 Paul talks about how he tries to always live a life with a clear conscious before God and man. When we are honest, we know when we are not in good conscious before God.

Testing the conscious is a great way to navigate through a life focused on fleshy desires verses life focused on spiritual living.

The best way to tell if you are in a battle with the flesh is to become disciplined at reading Scripture. God's spirit can speak back to your conscience what you have studied in his word. As you study his word you will read about behaviors that grieve God's Spirit, and there will be no question about certain acts of the flesh.

Second of all you will be strengthened in all areas of the dance. Hebrew 12 talks about strengthening feeble arms…. The only way to win against the flesh is to develop the strength to fight against it. When you first begin to focus on a new battle, the flesh may win. It's ok; we have a forgiving God who understands your weaknesses. Keep trying to strengthen your feeble arms.

When it comes to learning how to stand firm in a new area I envision a newborn lamb. It takes a great deal of determination and time for the baby lamb to begin to stand, but even then he will fall over. The baby lamb keeps trying to stand in spite of falling over repeatedly, until he can stand firm; but walking is another story. He may try to take some steps, but his back-end may come up off the ground. He may even lose control to the point that his back-end flips over his head. It takes time and effort, but soon the baby can run and jump and play. The whole process begins by his effort to strengthen his feeble legs, and then he must focus on learning to use them.

The same is true with our spiritual disciplines. Any war against the flesh begins with our feeble efforts that need to be strengthened. Our weakness is never an excuse to indulge. God expects us to grow from weak, to strong, from infantile to mature Christians. He is patient in our process but excuses we had when we were young in our walk with Christ should not still be used 10 years later. (Hebrews 5:12-6:2)

I love an analogy I have heard about how strengthening character is similar to working out. We all have muscles, though they are not visible on everyone. Lifting weights challenges the muscles, no matter how small and underdeveloped it is. The more you challenge a muscle the larger, firmer, and more developed it becomes. So too with your spiritual life, the more you are challenged in your spiritual life, the more you will grow. Learning to kill your flesh is about growing and developing in self-control and maybe even humility. Both are present, though you may not begin with much tolerance, but they can grow as you exercise them. At first you will fall short, but as time goes on you will find yourself more and more tolerant of sitting in the discomfort. The key to growing in killing the flesh is to learn to stand firm on God's truth, even when it is not easy.

One Final Word About Killing the Flesh

Sometimes our unhealthy habits, or self-indulgent behaviors make fighting the flesh even more difficult and may lead to consequences we may forever live with. For example there is a physiological high that is addicting when one indulges in looking at pornography. This high may result in making healthy sexuality seem boring and less satisfying. The self-indulgent behavior may have consequences that may take years to untangle. Unhealthy love affairs where there are highs and lows may lead to a dependency on the highs and lows for love to feel gratifying. There is an addictive chemical released inside the brain in certain unhealthy situations.

I compare it to the pattern of someone who suffers from Bi Polar depression. They live on polar opposites of a continuum. On one side there is a low that is so low they can barely function. It is hard to get out of bed for days, but as they move through the natural progression of Bipolar they come to the other end of the continuum where they hit euphoria. During this phase of the cycle the individual feels exhilaration and they may not sleep for days. They have high hopes and high dreams. They feel like they can take on the world and life is more than terrific. It is euphoria. They hit this high only to crash and land in despair once again. The low lows make the highs feel even better. For them, it is worth living through the lows to get to the highs.

Most of us cannot relate to a manic phase of life, but for the person with Bipolar, it's what they live for. Once they are put on medication the highs and lows balance out, however once you have experienced euphoria, normal feels bland. This is why so many people with Bipolar will go off of their medication. The euphoria is not healthy, it is dysfunctional, but it is fun.

The same thing can happen with life after unhealthy choices we make. Healthy may seem boring after the thrill of unhealthy, so the desire to leave a good husband for another exhilarating love affair with lots of ups and downs grows, a healthy sexual encounter in a respectful committed relationship pales in comparison to the pull of explicit pornography with graphic exploitation of women, a get together without free flowing alcohol seems dull. Sex completely sober feels bland. But it's healthy. Once you open doors that are meant to stay closed you may be in a battle to close those doors for years, or even for life. Healthy may pale in comparison to some of your unhealthy patterns of the past, but healthy leads to a more fulfilling life in the end.

You cannot avoid dancing around a dead man; you are one. But you can improve your dance as a new creation. Seek out God's truth and apply it. Learn self-denial and self- discipline. God knows where you struggle and he will bless your efforts to crucify the zombie inside.

I would like to close this chapter by encouraging you to take a few moments to reflect and pray about your flesh.

> In light of chapter 3, is there any area you are dancing without total authenticity? If so, where?
>
> How can you begin to address those areas?
>
> What are some of God's truths to stand on as you face your inauthentic places?

Here are a few Scriptures you may pull from for encouragement: Psalm 139, Jeremiah All of Psalm 51 but particularly verses 6, 10, 12, 15-17, Psalm 17:10, Luke 16:15, Isaiah 66:2

> In light of chapter 4, what are some of your shattered dreams?

> How have you danced through them?

> What are some truths you can cling to in your specific story?

Here are some Scriptures you may pull from for encouragement. Psalm 34:18-19, Psalm 147:3, Jeremiah 33:3, John 14:1, Isaiah 41:9-10

> In light of chapter 5 what are some of your idols?

> What are some things that maybe you wouldn't call idols, but could call vices, or props?

> What could you do to address these things?

> In light of chapter 6 what are some of the storms you have lived through?

> How did you handle some of them?

> How did you grow?

> Are there storms you are dancing through now? What are they?

How have you been handling them?

How can you improve dancing through the storms of the present and future?

"To turn the other cheek, is so hard when the other cheek is already bruised." ~Steve Camp; Forgive Me Forgive You

"Forgiveness is the fragrance that the violet sheds on the heel that has crushed it." ~Mark Twain

"Forgiveness is an attitude that says 'I will walk through life with a limp as a result of your actions and that is okay, because I recognize the damage cannot be undone no matter how much I demand it.' It is letting go of the need for vindication because words said cannot be unsaid, a violation cannot become un-violating. Forgiveness accepts that the situation is exactly what it is" ~Michele Kenney

Chapter 8
Dancing Among Wolves

Christians have a lot of ideas about forgiveness, but not many truly understand what true forgiveness really is. I remember the day that my mother and I were sitting in the sauna at the YMCA one afternoon after going for a swim. We were discussing a difficult situation I was facing that required not only forgiveness but also a genuine love towards someone who is not easy to love. While in the presence of this person, my character is consistently attacked, but even harder is that my children are continually compared to her own children. She finds faults in everything my children do, and she takes advantage of all opportunities to lift her own children up in comparison to mine. It hurts deeply. I have been put in a position where I am required to interact with this person on a very regular basis, and I am required to be kind to her and show love to her. There is no way out of this relationship. The fact that I don't "do fake" well means I have to find a way to love this person, and forgive her daily.

As my mother and I were discussing an upcoming event where I would have to be with this woman for an extended time, another woman entered the sauna. It was impossible for this woman not to over hear the conversation between my mother and me, and so at some point she entered into the conversation. She did not hesitate to reprimand me for my selfishness. She told me that I was commanded to love the other person, and forgiveness was required of me as a Christian. She reminded me of how much Jesus forgave me, and so this should not be a problem for me as a believer. It was my Christian duty and perhaps through my ability to show the other individual the love of Jesus, she would also become a believer. She let me know about a book written by an author I am very familiar with. I have read it and I cannot disagree with the version of forgiveness depicted in the book more.

Genuine forgiveness is not just a matter of pressing the hurt feelings down. Genuine forgiveness is a process that gets to the root of things. One of my beloved professors from Grace College, Tammy Schultz, co authored a book entitled "Beyond Desolate"*(1). The book is about healing from sexual abuse. Tammy addresses the topic of forgiveness using the analogy of cutting down weeds. See, if you decide to get rid of a field of weeds by simply cutting them at the stem, inevitably those weeds will grow back, and often times in a higher number. The only way to truly address a weed problem is to go deeper, you must start at the root.

But instead of going to the root for forgiveness, we try to rush it. We go with the quick fix and demand from ourselves, or others that we "forgive and forget". Many believe that quick forgiving and forgetting is a Biblical concept, but it isn't. Check it out for yourself. God says he separates our sin as far as the east is from the west, but we are not commanded to forgive and forget. Not only is this concept ridiculous, but also it is dangerous.

Just think of it this way, if I found out that Uncle Marvin had been molesting my daughter little Cindy, I should find my way to genuinely forgive him, but I would be a fool to forget and let him have access to her again. If Leah finds out her husband has been having multiple affairs on her and is not repentant for his sins against her, it is foolish for her to forgive and forget. Jumping back into bed with him puts her life at risk. Far too many times people allow themselves to be steam rolled over by bullies because they believe it is Biblical to forgive and forget.

 Another danger that can happen is a false version of forgiveness. Years ago I was walked through a session about freedom. There is nothing wrong with a sessions that help others find freedom, however if the facilitator is too passive about complex subjects like forgiveness, and tries to simplify it to "repeat after me" methods, it may be nothing more than a charade. The way I was "taught" to forgive was to say, "I forgive so and so for such and such. When they did what they did I felt a lot of pain. But as of today I release him and forgive him completely." That was it. All done. Check that duty off my list of important Christian tasks to accomplish. But in truth I had not done anything but recite words. It was almost as if I was taking a beach ball and holding it down under the water. I could fight it to stay below the surface, but it is a fight, it is not gone and eventually it may explode up to the surface. And inevitably with un-forgiveness that's exactly what happens, it explodes to the surface.

 So if these are not examples of forgiveness then what does it look like to forgive? We can find a perfect example of it with a parable Jesus tells in Matthew 18. It starts with a servant who is in debt to his king for 10 ten thousand talents. In today's terms this amount is the equivalence to $20 Million dollars. The king decided to settle his debts and this man was brought before him. When the servant told him he was unable to repay the debt, the king ordered that he, his wife, children and all he owned be sold to make up for the money owed. The servant fell face to the floor, and begged for mercy from the King. The King had mercy on this servant, and forgave the debt.

There are many great truths in this story but it requires just a bit more time to think about the lessons that can be found here than most of us give it. When money is loaned to someone, the lender no longer has the money that they once had. In a similar way when someone hurts us, we are no longer the same as we were before we were hurt. They have taken something from us. Like the servant in the story who would never have $20 million to give back to the King, those who have hurt us will never have whatever it is they took from us to give it back. Once words come out of someone's mouth, they can't unsay those words. Once someone has let you down in some way, they can't take back that time that they let you down, once a violation has occurred you cannot go back and un-violate. A father who abandoned his child for the first 10 years of his child's life cannot give those 10 years back. We are only left with choices about this type of emotional debt:

    #1 we can choose to demand payment for a debt owed to us for the rest of our lives when it cannot be paid, or

    #2 we can choose to forgive or let go of that debt, and understand that it will never be paid back, even if the violating person tries.

If we choose to demand repayment, we introduce a new problem into the situation. No amount of effort to make things right will truly satisfy the debt. As a result we take on the consequences of their violation against us.

I know I have "forgiven" people at times, yet still demanded they pay back the debt. The forgiveness was conditional. I had a set amount of conditions and standards that were needed to keep the offenses towards me just below the surface. I was happy when they were able to keep the conditions and standards. It was a false forgiveness that was established and things were peaceful for a time. But the moment they dropped the ball so to speak, I was angry at the old things all over again, and the new offenses were piled on top. I was demanding payment for a debt they could never repay. I began to understand that I needed to carry the consequence of the pain that their actions had caused me, it was mine to carry, they owe me nothing for the violations. Once I understood this, I became much easier to live with.

As We Forgive So Shall We Be Forgiven

There is more to the parable Jesus tells. The second part is about the forgiven servant and what he did next. After the King extended grace and mercy to this first servant, the servant immediately went out and found a fellow servant who owed him the equivalent of about a day's wage of money. The original servant began choke his fellow servant and demand the debt be paid back. The fellow servant begged for mercy the same as the original servant did, and he promised to pay it back, but the original servant had no mercy on him and had him thrown into jail.

When the king found out how the original servant handled his fellow servant he ordered the guards to get him and throw him into prison where he was to be tortured (Matthew 18:34)

Now let's take into perspective the representation of these people in this parable that Jesus gives. The King is representative of the King of King, Lord of Lords, God in Heaven. We all sin against God; we all owe him a big debt that we can never pay back. No matter how good we may think we are, our debt to God is unpayable when taken into consideration his holiness. He has never created a debt of his own to anyone. He has never been the author of any violation or offense ever in the history of man, and yet, in our 80 years of life, we are responsible for thousands, millions, maybe even billions of offenses that we may never even acknowledge, let alone beg forgiveness for. So let's say the original servant represents us. Many people will cause us offenses in our lives, sometimes intentional, sometimes unintentional. Let's call the fellow servant one of those people who will cause us offense in our lifetime. What right do we have to demand payment for so little, when we have been forgiven so much?

In the end, the first servant, the one initially forgiven by the king, is thrown into prison to be tormented. This may mean thrown into hell. After all, Matthew 6:14 says as we forgive, so shall we be forgiven. But I also believe that there is a psychological kind of torment that happens when we do not forgive. It has been said that un-forgiveness is where we drink poison expecting someone else to die. I have lived with un-forgiveness, and it is indeed very poisonous. In fact I would dare to say much of my "Psych-ache" and lack of peace in my early years were directly linked to areas I needed to forgive others. In other words, my un-forgiveness kept me in a psychological prison where I was tormented day and night.

We can change the way our story ends though if we choose to extend the same mercy upon our indebted as God has shown us. In fact we are commanded to.

Usually when we do not let someone else off the hook for a debt they owe us, it has everything to do with our own perspective. I know of a woman who was a survivor of sexual abuse. She and her husband waited until they were married to be sexually united, but then he violated her in the wedding bed time and time again. He used his patience before the ceremony as a weapon against her. As she cried during physical intimacy, he still took what he believed was his right, uncaring toward her feelings what so ever. Over time, she became hardened and bitter towards him.

Vicious verbal conflict erupted between the two of them on a regular basis. He hurt her with the way he treated her, she hurt him with her words. She tells of one Sunday after a toxic verbal exchange happened before church. During the praise and worship service at church, she felt God impressing on her spirit about how he cared and was holding her in her pain, almost like a "spiritual hug". At first she felt vindicated and comforted. The God of the universe understood how her husband hurt her, and he cared. But her vindication did not last long because by the time they finished singing that song, she also understood that God cared about the wounds she was also inflicting on her husband with her words towards him. She was a victim, but she was also victimizing.

I believe that in most relational problems, whether husband wife, parent child, co-workers friends, usually both parties victimize each other. There frequently is two-way responsibility where forgiveness is needed. Not in every case of course a child whom a family member is molesting has no responsibility to take, a woman who has been raped with physical force has no responsibility for what another person has done to her. But in most relational cases both parties can take responsibility.

For example, I am a survivor of domestic violence. For years I was bitter, and I put all responsibility on my ex husband. I refused to offer him forgiveness and it kept me in emotional bondage, more on that in a moment. It was not until I began to accept responsibility for the role I played in my circumstances that I began to heal emotionally. See, I wanted that relationship, despite direct warnings from people who loved me. I pursued that relationship even when doors were closing. He had proven his character, yet I chose to enter into a marital commitment to him. Three years later when I was healing from the physical and emotional scars, and he was off with the girlfriend he had been cheating on me with, I couldn't understand what had gone wrong. I had responsibility in that trouble I got myself into. Before true healing could take place, I had to forgive myself as well as him.

Beyond taking responsibility for where we may contribute to the problem, or where we may be victimizing our victimizer is also the fact that we are forgiven by God. Let me bring up another story we find in Scripture to put this into perspective.

A man came to this earth, born of a virgin. This man was no ordinary man; he was fully man, fully God. He chose to leave his beautiful home of perfection, just to live among his created. He wanted to know us as we are, but he also knew there was only one way this fallen creation of his could have restoration of his original dream. He knew there was one way we could enter a relationship with him and his

Father. There was nothing his creation could do to pay back the debt owed to him and his father. Innocent blood had to be shed. And so because of his intense love for us he was tortured, and murdered so his own innocent blood could pay our debts to a perfect loving God. He bore the consequences of our debt to him. If you have accepted that perfect innocent blood for the forgiveness of your sins, then is it fair to say that same blood was not enough to forgive the sins of your own debtor? Truly, there is no room for you not to have mercy on someone else.

The Different Kinds of Forgiveness

In the book "Beyond Desolate"*(1), Tammy Schultz names the three types of forgiveness found in Scripture. Understanding what forgiveness is, and the different kinds of forgiveness may be helpful for you as you follow Christ's lead while dancing through forgiveness. The first kind of forgiveness is judicial. This is what Christ gives us through his blood when we confess we have sinned and we acknowledge that we are not able to pay back the debt we owe him. We have violated him; he has the right to judge; yet he pardons us (Romans 6:23).

The second kind is psychological forgiveness. This is simply for the benefit of the individual who extends forgiveness. It does not require reconciliation. In Acts 15:36-40 we read that Paul and Barnabas have a conflict so intense that they split company. I am certain that they forgave each other, were kind to one another, yet it appears they agreed it would best for each to go their separate ways permanently.

Let's look again at the scenario illustrated above. If Uncle Marvin is molesting little Cindy, the best kind of forgiveness is psychological forgiveness, not the kind that reconciles the relationship. Insisting on forgiveness and relational reconciliation is unsafe for little Cindy. Even if Uncle Marvin changes, it may be psychologically victimizing to Suzie every time she interacts with him.

How many times do Christians expect other Christians to

be victims in the name of Jesus? I think it happens a lot, especially in the case of marriage. When an oath of marriage has been taken, the expectation is that someone who is truly seeking God will stay no matter what. But what is to be done in the case of abuse? Can't God redeem? Certainly he can, but will he? He can heal cancer too, but he doesn't always, so too in serious marital problems. This is a fine line and anyone dealing with their own abusive situation, or helping another individual in an abusive marital situation needs to be very cautions in their advising or moves.

    We are called to love others as we love ourselves. Is it loving oneself to continually be subject to another's person's abuse of our will, body, spirituality, emotion or mind? In the same way we are required to love them. Is it loving to allow bad behavior to go unchecked? Even God Himself disciplines those he loves. If we carry someone else's consequence on our backs do we truly love them? Do we truly love ourselves?

    Unconditional love has conditions. Jesus loves us all unconditionally, yet he says "You may only reap the benefits of relationship with me if you abide in me. If you reject my teaching, I will love you, but I will not be in relationship with you (John 3:16, John 14:21-24, 1 John 4)." It is clear in Scripture that sin separates us from God (Is. 59). It puts a hold on the relationship if we are caught up in perpetual un-repentant sin. Should this be the same in harmful behaviors within a marriage? These are very important questions to explore in cases of forgiveness when there are forms of abuse present.

    The final form of forgiveness is the kind that leads to reconciliation. This kind of forgiveness does attempt to forgive and forget, or at least put it fully out of the way of relationship. No longer will the violation be used as a weapon. Depending on the violation, this kind of forgiveness may take time. Time is needed if the root of the pain is to be exposed and dealt with. When done correctly, the kind of forgiveness that leads to reconciliation is a process and it requires patience.

All of the versions of forgiveness, even the psychological kind recognized that we are all sinners. I am no better than any of my violators. Does it matter if I don't violate others the same as I have been violated? Does it matter that I have never cussed someone out, physically assaulted someone, or even murdered someone? If I look hard enough there will always be someone worse than me. Does it matter? I still have violated God and I am still in need of forgiveness. I am no better than other violators. We are all wolves dancing amongst wolves. We all need to be forgiven, just as we need to forgive.

*(1) Sourced in back

"But the master of deception now begins with his dissection of the Word and with all of his craft and subtly the serpent twists the simple truths they've heard." ~Don Fransisco; Adam Where are You

"The enemy of my soul says your holding out on me."~Time In-between, Francesca Battistelli

Satan is a liar, and he wants to make us think that we are paupers, when he knows himself we are children of the King" ~The Imperials; Praise the Lord

Chapter 9
Dancing Against the Enemy

In the movie the Tourist(1), European authorities are looking for their enemy, Alexander Pierce. Pierce is a thief who has stolen millions of dollars from the country and other people. In the midst of avoiding arrest, he has committed several crimes leading to the status of most wanted in Europe. The problem the authorities are having is that Pierce is crafty. He had plastic surgery and changed his identity to counterfeit as an American man named Frank. Pierce always seems to be one step ahead of the police. To make matters more frustrating, he has seduced one of their top female agents. She plays both sides protecting him, and looking to catch him. As one character put it, "She doesn't know what side she is on."

At one point in the movie the authorities have Pierce in their custody posing as "Frank". They are unaware of his true identity. They did not arrest him because he broke any laws, but simply because he is, in their minds, an annoyance that they need to keep out of their way. The worst part is that the only reason the authorities caught him was because it was all part of Pierce's master plan to get away with his crimes and gain ground on the police.

This scenario goes against the American military's motto to "know your enemy." If you don't know who your enemy is, what your enemy looks like, the tactics of your enemy, or how your enemy tries to attack, your enemy will win against you every time. The damage an enemy with this kind of advantage has the potential to do, is devastating. Think about Pearl Harbor, The Oklahoma City Bombing, or 9-11. All of these were surprise attacks where the enemy was unknown or underestimated, but the results were life changing and grievous.

I see a parallel of this movie and real life. We also have an enemy. He is real and he is tactful. Most Christians do not know this enemy. In a poll taken in 2009 by a organization called Barna*(2), it was found that 40% of professing Christians do not believe Satan exists, and an additional 36% were either unsure if they believed, or had mixed thoughts on his existence. Only 26% of professing Christians in the survey conducted by Barna strongly believed in Satan's existence. This poll only addresses Christians. I would imagine these numbers are even higher among non-believers. The fact is, the enemy of mankind's soul is our enemy whether we believe in God or not.

Since so many people do not recognize our enemy, he is wreaking havoc on our society. Many Christians have been seduced to the point that it is hard to know which side they are on. Others are hanging out in his company because they are unfamiliar that they are keeping company with the enemy, some may see him as a mild annoyance but they don't take him as the serious threat he is. I want to take a moment to familiarize you with the enemy of your soul.

Who is Satan?

Here in America, we have our little jokes about the devil. He is portrayed as a little guy with horns and a pointy tail and a pitchfork. He is almost even cute in some of the ways he is portrayed. We play with evil, we walk as close to the line without falling over, we dabble in things with the mindset that some evil is innocent or fun. Some examples could be Halloween, scary movies, spiritualism, slasher films, and music that dis-respects life or sexuality. But according to Scripture Satan is far from the cute little guy we see depicted in cartoons, and anything connected to him is dangerous to us. Taking evil lightly for the sake of entertainment is bad idea no matter how you look at it.

The truth is Satan hates you. He hates everything about you and he is out to destroy you. He hates you because he hates God. Satan is a defeated foe; he knows his rebellion has closed the door to any second chances with God. If he is going down he wants to take as many with him as he can. He obviously cannot take God down but he knows how to hurt God, and that is by attacking the "apple of His eye" (Zachariah 2:8; Psalm 17:8).

If you have children you know what I mean here. If you really want to hurt me, hurt my kids. Recently a friend of mine was blown away by my behavior. We were in the midst of a situation where someone had hurt me with their actions and words. My friend was mad at the circumstance, I on the other hand, was pretty placid about the entire thing, and immediately was speaking forgiveness and understanding into the situation.

During that same day another situation arose involving my son. He had made some very poor choices. My heart was grieving at the what he had done, but I found out that other boys who had done the exact same things, along with their family members were "throwing verbal stones" at my son. The only difference between my son and these other boys was that my son was the only one who had gotten caught. I was infuriated. I was ready to go over and pick a fight. My friend was baffled at how one individual had sinned against me and I was ok with it, but when my son was sinned against I was ready to get physical. There is special kind of pain involved when your children are being hurt. Satan knows this, and he takes full advantage of it with God's created children.

Scripture says that God is love. This means that God doesn't just love us; it means everything about his character is love. Everything that God does is immersed in love.

Satan is the opposite of God. He wants nothing to do with God's character, his goodness or his love. Satan hates you. Everything he does is to destroy you, but he is tactful in his approach. He is patient in his schemes, deceitful, tricky, crafty. Though he is a defeated foe, he is dangerous. He should not be taken lightly, yet we treat him as though he is a joke. It's like playing with a lion as if it were a cute little kitten.

There are several ways we take Satan lightly. In this chapter I hope to give you a better understanding of him, and how to battle against him. I also hope to explain how important it is to be on guard so we don't get deceived. We need to know our enemy is real, and know who he is. We need to stop underestimating him. It is time for Christians to learn about our fight against the enemy.

Know Our Enemy

Satan is a created being who is walking in rebellion against God. There are several Scriptures in the Bible that talk about him. Isaiah and Ezekiel both have Scriptures that tell a story that some Bible scholars say clearly portray Satan's fall, while others say these Scriptures are only talking about earthly kings. I do not want to be too arrogant in my stance on it, but I find the descriptions interesting and fitting to what may have played out before the dawn of time. The possible description of Satan basically states that Satan (who at the time likely had a different name since Satan literally means the adversary) was created as a very high positioned angel. He held a lot of power and status in heaven, but he wanted more. He wanted God's throne and he wanted to be worshipped above God and so he began a rebellion. This rebellion resulted in his getting thrown out of heaven along with every angel that wanted to follow him, 1/3 of the heavenly beings.

Again, scholars disagree on whether this story truly is about Satan, however it does line up with what other Scriptures say about him. We do know that Satan has a kingdom (Matt. 12:26), and he has heavenly beings that follow him (Matt 12:24; Matt 25:41).

Regardless of how all things came into play we also know this about him; he was a liar from the beginning. When he lies he speaks his native tongue. He is a murderer. The truth is not in him. All of this come from the words of Jesus himself in John 8:44. We also know he is crafty and scheming (Gen 3:1;Eph 6:11;2 Tim. 2:26). He disguises himself to appear to be righteous (2 Cor 2:10-11; 2 Thes 2:9-10). He uses what God says, but twists it just enough to lead us into sin (Gen 3:4; Luke 4:1-12). He will slip into a body of believers, appearing to be one of them, but his intent is destruction (Acts 20:28-30;2 Peter 2:1-3;Matt24:4-5;Matt7:15; Romans 16:17-18).

1 Peter 5:8 says to "Be sober-minded; be watchful. Your adversary the devil prowls around like a roaring lion, seeking someone to devour." Devour! Please understand the severity of that word. The Greek word used in this context is *Katapiein*.

Katapiein means to devour drink down, gulp down, drown, swallow (up).

English translation of devour is to destroy, consume, take in eagerly, to prey on.

The Greek word for seek used in this text is *zeteo* it means to seek, specially, (by Hebraism) to worship (God), or (in a bad sense) to plot (against life) (I am guessing this is the context meant in 1 Peter 5:8).

Visualize this with me if you will. Your enemy, the accuser, your advisory, the deceiver who schemes and disguises himself, prowls around like a hungry roaring lion. How do you suppose a lion looks when he is hungry? When he is seeking out his prey, plotting against the life of his next meal? I know the text says roaring, which in itself is enough to sober me up and take notice, but a lion who has found his prey and is now on the hunt is no longer roaring, he is stealthy, quiet, and he tries very hard not to bring attention to himself. He does his best to blend into the dry Sahara brush before he makes his attack. According to some people a lion will roar when he is in the midst of an attack to strike a paralyzing fear into them. I did not see credible confirmation on that, but in the case of Satan it can be true. He will try to strike fear in your soul. When a lion gets his prey he devours it. All of it. Remember the earlier definition? A lion leaves no shred of his victim.

Does this sound comparable to a cute little red guy with horns? Does he seem like a little plaything? Does it sound like anything that is connected to him could ever be innocent? It can be fun, no doubt, but his version of fun always has a dangerous agenda. Paul warns to be sober minded so you don't fall victim to this lion. A real lion can only kill your body, but this one wants to lead you down a path of destruction that will kill your soul.

Sneak Attacks

I once worked with a man who I thought shared my beliefs in God. We would have long talks about God and his goodness on our breaks. I began to look forward to our talks since we were to only two believers in my workplace; at least I thought so for a very long time. We talked about God the Father, and his Son Jesus. It seemed we were on the same page, until one day he mentioned something that sparked further talk about this "god" he worshiped.

He told me that he really didn't read the Bible much anymore, but there was a book series he had read that helped him understand god at a much better level. He told me he wanted to help me out by giving me this book. The author was man who had became very angry with God. From the sounds of it, he had been practicing "religion", which I hope by now you are beginning to understand that the dance with Christ is less about religion and more about relationship with him. Anyway, he had grown weary of keeping the rules and he began to get angry with God. One day (I believe he was in his car) he began to yell at God about how hard it is to find him and know him. It was during his outpour of resentment that "god" began to talk to him.

The man was told to write down everything this "god" was telling him. It took up three books and he was able to publish all three of them. My friend gave me the first book. I began to read it, already understanding it was of Satan, but I wanted to know what it said. I could not read for long, the content made me sick. See, I grew up in a Christian home, and though at that time in my life I was not the studier of God's word that I am now, I had a pretty good foundation, one that many people do not have early on in their dance. If I were more naive, I easily could have been deceived. It all sounded good, it all sounded like truth. There was enough Scriptural reference, and Scriptural truth in it to sound good, but at the core it was evil.

I don't remember much about what was in that book, but I do remember the last thing I read. It was enough to chill me to the bone and it was enough for me to put the book down and never pick it up again except to put it in the trash. I wish I had burned it.

In Exodus 3 God is instructing Moses to begin to process of leading the Israelites out of captivity from the Egyptians. Moses asks God who he should tell the Israelites sent him on this mission and God responds in 3:14 by saying: "I AM WHO I AM. This is what you are to say to the Israelites: 'I AM has sent me to you.'"

There was a place in the book where the author asks the "god" who is speaking to him, "Who are you?" and the reply was, "I am what I am not." Even as I recount this story in written word 7 years later, the eeriness returns. This is plenty of evidence of how our enemy uses craftiness to take God's light and twist it into distortion, but even still I can give you another example of his craftiness from much more recent.

We had a guest over to our house yesterday. This young man is new to the Lord and let me tell you he is hungry to know more about

God and how to follow him. Rarely do I see such hunger for Godliness, but this man is starving. He grew up without much truth around him, and he was encased with heartache after heartache. Since coming to Christ he knows for sure that there is something evil about a Weegie board, so he stays away from them, but somehow he had something called an Angel Board. He didn't think it could be evil because of the name.

We had been on the topic of witchcraft and weegie boards. He spoke boldly against all spiritualism and things Satanic. There was something else he wanted to add to the conversation, but suddenly his mind went blank. He couldn't remember what he wanted to say. He was really frustrated that he couldn't remember. Silently I prayed and asked God to help him remember if it was important. Immediately after my prayer this young man was able to remember that he wanted to tell us about his experience with the Angel board. He told us how wonderful it was to ask angels about things of the unknown, and to get answers from God's perspectives unlike with a Weegie board. We were able to converse about how an angel board is also a dangerous thing to play with. Scripture is clear about speaking to all spirits (Deut. 18:10) but as a new believer he would not know that.

Satan is able to block us in our journey, and block rescue (1 Thes. 2:18; Daniel 10:13). I believe in the same way our spiritual enemy was able to block that young man's thought process to try to keep him deceived (1 Thes. 2:18; Daniel 10:13). He is able to mess with our minds. He is able to put thoughts there, or to make us sleepy or distracted when we read Scripture. This is called spiritual oppression. Our enemy starts a battle with us outside of our bodies, but using our minds or circumstances to wage war against us.

The author Neil Anderson has several books on this subject if you want to read more on it. You can also see a very good depiction of how Satan appears as an angel of light by reading to book "The Beautiful Side of Evil",*(3) a story of a woman caught up with a "gifting" to see and interact with spirits. She was in the middle of training with a psychic healer when she became more aware of Jesus Christ. Every time she tried to read her Bible an oppressive sleepiness would come over her. Finally, she asked for God to reveal the power behind her own power, and reveal it he did. She saw the demonic gifting for what it was. Not beautiful, but hideous.

Satan is out to look as much like God as possible, but he stands for the opposite. At the heart of Christian beliefs is a desire to pursue God and his truth. We seek out love and selflessness, holiness and purity. Not all people know that there is a religion that is opposite of Christianity. The religion of Satanism pursues hate and selfishness, it is intentionally opposite to anything God says. Occultism is the worship of Satan and his powers. Some think there is not such thing as these religions, they are just made up to scare people, but both exist and both are dangerous. I believe Satan planted the lie that these are made up religions to keep Christians in the dark, and to give him more power to keep deceiving our world.

Satan tries to counterfeit God in other ways too; it's not just in religion. There is the Godhead Trinity; Father, Son Holy Spirit. Revelation is clear that in the last days, Satan will have his own trinity as well; Dragon (Satan), Beast (The Anti-Christ), (The false prophet). He will use his craftiness to appear as much like God as possible in order that he may lead you astray. It is important to look for those tiny discrepancies between God's statutes and those of the Satanic agenda. He is sneaky, he is crafty, and he does have power to deceive. Deceit is his strongest weapon. We can only discern Satan's craftiness by dancing closely to our Savior, and looking to Christ for his wisdom and power.

The Bloody Battle

Satan does not always appear so beautiful. Sometimes he wages a full out war against God's saints. These wars will leave you spiritually and emotionally bleeding. They are wounding and painful attacks. An example of this is perhaps most evident in the book of Job, where Satan appears to God with other spiritual beings. God asks him where he had come from, and Satan replies "From roaming throughout the earth, going back and forth on it." The depicted scene is actually congruent with scripture that says Satan roams to and fro seeking whom he may devour.

God does something curious here, he asks Satan if he had considered his servant Job, a good upright man. Satan takes God's challenge about his servant's steadfast heart toward God, and begins to wage a war against Job with the intent to cause him to fall. He can do nothing without God's permission, but Satan is the one doing the attack. In the end, when Job has stood firm, God blesses him and gives back much of what was taken away, but not all. Satan took his children from Job, though he had more children, more children would not replace those taken from him. Much was restored, but ultimately Job walks the rest of this life with a limp of grief. Some of the things Satan steals away will forever leave scars.

Recently, I went through a situation that I knew had to be an all out war against me. But in some ways it didn't make sense to me that it could have been Satan. It seemed too sneaky, and yet too obvious. I was praying questioning if Satan had the kind of authority to deceive when deceit was being prayed against, and to attack as aggressively when protection is the request. The answer I received from God was an absolute yes. I realized through research and God's revelation that there are ways that Satan can attack even when the situation is covered in prayer. I want to name and briefly discuss the four areas that Satan will wage a spiritually bloody war against God's people.

Testing

The first is what was discussed with above with Job. Satan asks God to take a steadfast servant of God and attack him. In the scenario of Job, he did not do anything wrong to lead to it, it was not a specific weakness that Satan was taking advantage of, it was not provoked or out of disobedience that this attack occurred. It was simply to see if Satan could make him fall. There are no firm answers on why God volunteered Job, but I speculate that it may have been to first of all put Satan's cockiness about God's people in check, and second though it seems odd, it was to honor Job. Think about it, Satan was talking smack about Job's reasons for loving God. God basically said, "Job is not that shallow. He is the real deal and if you don't believe me test him. He will indeed, show his true colors when life heats up for him, and his character will come out. But I'm telling you his character is solid. He will not turn his back on me because you throw difficult circumstances his way."

Satan on the other hand scoffed at God's confidence in Job. But in the end, who was right? Satan was arrogant in his stance but proven wrong. I believe the same can happen with us. God can give Satan permission to test us. But in the end he follows our faithfulness with blessings and stronger character.

Sifting

In Luke 22:31 Peter is told that Satan has asked to sift him (and the others) like wheat. At first I struggled a little to figure out what is the difference between what happened to Job and Peter. Sifting is a shaking, in order that a separation occurs. The dead will fall off, the bulky will remain. In both cases I'm sure "dead things" fell off from their personalities. Satan was hoping that the bad character would be the stronger part of their personality, and it would be the faith that fell. But for both Job and Peter, the good character remained and ugliness in their character died and fell away.

It was in the stories themselves that I can see what is different between Job and Peter. Job was minding his own business; his testing came about as a conversation between God and Satan. Peter was an instrument of God; Satan's hope was to stop the work God had for Peter. Furthermore Satan went straight for the "holes in Peter's armor". He knew Peter's weaknesses and he successfully played into those weaknesses. I strongly believe that after Peter fell by denying his Lord three times on the night of his death, Satan put thoughts into his head that emotionally beat him up; thoughts that called him a coward, and asked him how God could ever use him now. Thoughts to try to paralyze the ministry God had for Peter. But Peter did not fall away.

Think about it this way, Peter was guilty of a form of betrayal, not as severe as Judas', but it was still painful disloyalty to his friend. Judas handled his version of betraying Jesus by committing suicide. Peter found redemption. In Judas' sifting all potential of redemption fell off, he did not try to seek forgiveness, he sought a way out through suicide. Judas' sifting ended in the tragedy Satan hoped it would. But with Peter's sifting, came healing and redemption, the result God hopes for when we are sifted. Peter had roots that went deeper than Judas'. The important thing to pray for during a sifting is deep-roots in Christ.

The Thorn

In 2 Corinthians 12:7-10 Paul writes about a thorn in his flesh, a "tormentor of evil". We have no idea what this thorn is, though there has been speculation. Some scholars have said perhaps it had to do with poor eyesight, leftover issues from when God blinded him. Others have said as a single man perhaps he struggled with lust. This one to me seems a little more plausible than cataracts, yet he instructs others to marry if they are burning with lust, and recommends that if possible one should stay single. It's also been theorized that he lived with guilt for killing many Christians. It's very possible that living with guilt was his struggle and I tend to lean toward that idea even though Paul talks a lot about living free from guilt. I know as a teacher of God's word, it is easy to teach, but living it out is sometimes more tricky. In fact, as already quoted in this book he as much as admits to it in (Romans 7:17-25).

The details of the thorn are not important. Perhaps the actual thorn was left out so all of us can relate to Paul, no matter what the thorn is that we struggle with. As humans we tend to rate things whether it be sins, circumstances, struggles, or thorns. Maybe the exact thorn is left out so someone whose struggle is with pornography doesn't feel less than Paul, or someone who is struggling with a harsh tongue doesn't feel superior to him.

What is important is that Paul pleads with God three times to take away the tormenting thorn, but God's only response is, "My grace is sufficient for you." In other words God says, "No. Taking away your struggle may cause you to fall into sin less, but your perfection is not a requirement to get into heaven…I knew that you could not be perfect which is why I sent Jesus. Taking away your thorn may make you more comfortable, but comfort is not what you are to be striving for. Taking away your thorn may make things easier for you, but I never promised you an easy life. No, my grace, the undeserved gift of your salvation, is good enough for you. Be content with that. Because of your thorn, my glory and strength is revealed even more."

Paul is clear, the thorn is a tormentor of Satan, but when God in his sovereignty does not take away your thorn, there is always a purpose for it. Paul is clear that he understands the purpose of his thorn is to keep him humble, and it is to show his weakness so that God's strength can be revealed in spite of it.

Paul was a mighty man of God, full of wisdom and used greatly by God. It would have been easy for him to take on some credit, or to become prideful in the way God was using him. I know myself, when God begins to use me I get excited and I feel fulfilled. Perhaps one of my many thorns may be that I get doors slammed in my face before I get too far in ministry. Otherwise I think I could easily slowly become more puffed up and prideful instead of innocently excited. This thorn has kept me humble thus far, and I believe the doors will continue to close until I am spiritually mature enough to handle God's use of my gifting.

Another potential thorn could be an itch of addiction. The itch means they don't indulge, but the desire is strong. It may be a relational struggle, a burden, or a roadblock. Regardless, the thorn is painful, unyielding, it reveals weakness, and it is a messenger of Satan. God gives permission for the thorn for his own purpose, but the thorn has a purpose beyond God's. It is to discourage you enough to turn you away from God. It is to expose your weakness in a way that your weakness is revealed not God's strength. This is a long lasting painful battle to fight against the enemy.

Handed Over For the Purpose of Redemption

The heart of man knows how to deceive itself. Unchecked we can get ourselves into trouble, no enemy needed. But our enemy has studied us for generations. When we are in a battle with our flesh, he knows we are in a weak moment. Just like the lion goes for the weak gazelle, the spiritual lion goes for us in our moments of weakness. It's amazing what stories human beings can come up with to justify behavior we don't want to change.

I was leading a weekend retreat for women. The theme was about freedom in Christ vs. Slavery to the idols we fashion to our likings. One woman attending, was desperate to speak to all of the leaders. She did not want to confess to us that she was neck deep in addiction, she wanted to let us all know that God had given the addiction to her and he was ok with it.

Two times Paul addresses situations where people are caught up in some form of blatant sin, where they are unrepentant and even excusing their behavior. The First time is found in 1 Corinthians 5 where a spiritual brother is involved in a sexual sin. The other is found in 1 Timothy 1:19-20 where two brothers are blaspheming. Paul's remedy in both situations is to hand them over to Satan so that they can learn the very hard lesson of playing games in the devils territory. The thought behind this action is that they will have a temporary personal destruction but in the end they will be brought to repentance.

During my rebellious days, my mom gleaned an analogy for me from the movie of The Lion King(4). Simba, the child of the King, was told to stay out of the elephant graveyard. But Simba was intrigued, even more so when his father sternly told him to stay away from it. He wanted to do what he wanted to do. Zazu was assigned to keep an eye on him, but regardless of all attempts to reason with Simba, he wanted to go exploring there anyway. Simba's persistence to go exploring beyond the clearly marked boundaries of his fathers kingdom resulted in an encounter with hyena's that almost took Simba's life. Simba had to go out of the care of his father before he learned the importance of obedience to his father. The same often is true for us. We need to be handed over to our sin, and allowed to do our own thing before we learn we are safer obeying God. Needless to say, Simba never wanted to play in the enemy's territory again.

God's intention of handing us over to our sin is not to destroy us, but to teach us. "Let them do what they will do, let Satan have them, hopefully the result of their sin will be so painful they will come to redemption." These are battles we choose to walk into. They are battles that are preventable and they may be the bloodiest battles of all.

Fighting the Enemy

Like it or not, we are engaged in a battle at all times. I saw a blog where the author insisted we are not in a battle. He states that God is more powerful than Satan, He threw Satan out of heaven, and all it will take is God's breath on Satan to permanently annihilate him. This may be true, but for whatever reason, God has chosen to allow the conflict of good and evil to play out. God has the final authority, but he has his reasons to allow Satan to proclaim war on his people. The blogger states we have no reason to show caution when it comes to the enemy of our souls. Nothing can be farther from the truth, and a mindset like that is dangerous.

Scripture clearly identifies the conflict between mankind and Satan as a battle; here are a few of the most common Scriptures that speak about our battle with Satan, about victory, and about Christians being conquerors etc....

Romans 8:36 we are more than conquerors through Christ Jesus

2 Timothy 2:3-4 Endure hardships like a good soldier, aim to please God your commanding officer

1 John 5:4 through faith we will have the victory

2 Corinthians 10:3-5 we wage war, but a different kind than the world wages. We use weapons with divine power that demolish things contrary to God.

1 Timothy 6:12 Fight the good fight of faith

1 Peter 2:11 Sin wages war against your soul

Revelation The entire book is about a war between God and his people against Satan.

Ephesians 6:12 our struggle is not against flesh and blood, but against the rulers, authorities, against the powers of this dark world and against the forces of evil in the heavenly realms.

Ephesians 6:10-18 we are in a spiritual war, there is spiritual armor that must always be in place, stand your ground.

Our God is a God of peace and order, but according to Scripture we are going to fight a battle against evil until the day of Christ's return. We are never to let down our guard. We must always be ready for an attack. Sometimes we have moments of peace, sometimes we simply need to be alert, but here are a couple things to keep in mind to help you know for sure a full out attack is underway. Our God is a God of peace (2 Thess. 3:16), if Satan is the opposite then we know he is the god of turmoil. Wherever there is friction, discord, anxiety, or anything that opposes peace you know there is some form of battle waging against you.

God is also a God of order (1 Cor 14:33). Have you ever been in a situation where there is peace and order and then suddenly chaos and confusion breaks out? I have. In fact in one particular situation I was in the midst of a ministering conference. A plan was set, we thought we all knew what was supposed to happen, but suddenly none of the leaders knew what was going on, some leaders misunderstood what the plan was. The only way to describe the situation is that sudden chaos and confusion broke out. At the same time one woman attending the weekend retreat was under some form of spiritual attack. We all stopped, and prayed for order to come back to the situation. You don't have to be in the midst of ministering for this to happen though. There have been times chaos breaks out in my home, conflict, bickering, and confusion all at once. This is a good time to take a break and begin a to get your battle plan for a counter attack against the enemy.

There are also times that we pray, God responds, and our enemy blocks God's messengers (Daniel 10) And times Satan will attempt to block us when we are doing God's work (1 Thess. 2:18). And of course there are the times we need God's protection from his deceit, and schemes. So how do we fight off our enemy? The conclusion that I have come to has actually been a bit of a revelation to me. In the past I have followed the lead of many Christians who speak boldly against the enemy, yelling at him, and reminding him he has lost his power. Christians like to tell him he is a defeated foe. But this is not Scriptural. Jude verses 8-10 says:

> *"In the very same way these dreamers pollute their own bodes,*

> *Reject authority, and slander celestial beings. But even the*
> *Archangel Michael, when he was disputing over the body of*
> *Moses, did not dare to bring slanderous accusations against*
> *him, but said, "The Lord rebuke you!" Yet these men speak*
> *Abusively against whatever they do not understand by instinct*
> *Like unreasoning animals–These are the very things that destroy*
> *Them."*

This is a warning. We do not need to engage in much verbal confrontation with the enemy of our souls; in fact to do this is foolishness. It invites the enemy to wage war against us. I remember when I first became aware that there was a spiritual enemy. I was probably around the age of 11 or 12. My parents had begun to minister to a young man who was under spiritual attack, and in fact he was likely possessed as a result of playing Dungeons and Dragons.

My parents had not engaged me in conversation about it; I was too young to really understand. But I had overheard my parents talking about Neil Anderson, spiritual warfare, and this young man. It peaked my interest and I began to ask questions. My mother carefully tried to answer them, but again, I was so young. I remember one part of the conversation that went something like this:

> **Me:** "So there are demonic spirits all around us that we can't see?"
> **My Mom:** "Yes"
> **Me:** "And if I pray for God to bind them, then they are unable to get loose?"

My Mom: "Yes"
Me: "Huh. That's cool"

I do believe some sort of warning followed the conversation, but I was so young, I didn't understand. Besides, my personality always has to try out the things I am warned against to see if it really is bad as bad as I was told it is. I must get that from my ancestor Eve. Anyway, after our conversation my mom went to the basement to do laundry and I began to taunt the evil spirits in my home. I said things out loud like,

> *"I bind you all in the name of Jesus Christ. Ha-ha, you cannot get me now. You are bound and unable to get unbound in the name of Jesus. How does that feel, you defeated foes!!"*

It seemed to work out well for me at first. I was on a power trip, and demons were bound. But starting that night the enemy of my soul began it's plan to lash back at me. I was terrified. A horrible, terrifying, paralyzing fear came over me. Thoughts swirled around in my head.

> *"Not so tough now are you"*
> *"We will get you"*
> *"Just wait until you fall asleep"*
> *"Did you hear that noise in your closet?"*
> *"Look at the shadows on the walls, are they moving?"*

I was plagued by fear at night for years. When I became a teenager it got to the point that I would be paralyzed, unable to move or speak. I would feel the fear enter my body and spread throughout it. It was not until I truly found Jesus in my mid 20's and he set me free from a lot of bondage and fear that I was finally relieved of this torment. But you see, it started by me speaking abusively of things I did not understand. I slandered celestial beings. And it led to a form of bondage. We must be careful when engaging in Spiritual Warfare.

If we are not to speak abusively against celestial beings, then what do we do? The first thing we must do is daily put on the full armor of God found in Ephesians 6:10-18. This is our spiritual protection against the attacks of the enemy.

The first piece of armor is the belt of truth. We have already established that Satan's native tongue is deceit. The best way to fight off lies is by stating the truth. There are a lot of voices calling out to us in this world, but we must seek out and listen to the voice of truth, and let it surround us the way a belt surrounds us. It is important to remember that truth rarely comes to you with out an act of deliberation to find it. In a world full false information, lies, and a value system based on relevance we must seek out truth and cling to it.

The next piece of armor is breastplate of righteousness. A physical breastplate wraps around your body. It is meant to protect vital organs such as your heart and lungs. These are the areas of your body that if damaged severely enough, would drain you of your life; so too with your breastplate of righteousness. When you are living a righteous life, perusing God's holiness your heart and vital spiritual "organs" are protected from the filth that will drain you of your spiritual vitality. But if you keep company with trouble makers, get drunk, listen to music that disrespects God's laws or human life you compromise your spiritual life. Your vital organs like your heart will be compromised towards God's righteousness.

Our feet must always have on them the readiness of the Gospel of Peace. For the longest time I didn't understand what this really means. How does this play into warfare? I believe in part it has to do with continually offering people the truth of God in a peaceful manner. Stern rebukes can be damaging, so our readiness must be cloaked in peace. But the other day I believe I gained a new insight to this. We must also have feet that are ready to obey God's direction. As stated before we are to stand firm, but sometimes there is a time for action. If we act too quickly we can cause a disaster, an example of this may be if I know someone needs to hear a convicting truth. If I move on my own will and need for control, I may cause a lot of damage to my friendship to no avail. But if God is working on my friend and he directs me to have a hard conversation, I must be willing to obediently move when God directs me. Battles of Satanic bondages can be won if the battle is of God, rather than my own human effort.

Next we have to take up the shield of faith. Taking up is a statement of action. Once we have faith it does not maintain itself. It is something that requires us to keep it up surrounding us. The shield that Paul had in mind would have been a very heavy shield I have read estimates of anywhere between 10 and 20 pounds. This may not sound like a lot, but think about being in warfare, fighting, and blocking using a 15 pound shield. Eventually it would take a lot of strength to block the flaming arrows constantly being launched at you. Paul says the purpose of the shield of faith is to extinguish the flaming arrows of the enemy. He throws all kinds of things at us to get us to question our faith. "Is God real?" "What if I am believing the wrong things?" "If God exists why did my prayer go unanswered?" These are all examples of the flaming arrows we need to block. But in warfare, that shield may become heavy, and we may be tempted to let the shield down. When thoughts of doubt penetrate our armor it is with no small consequence. Satan has succeeded in penetrating your armor of righteousness, leaving holes of vulnerability that he can and will take full advantage of.

We are to put on the helmet of salvation. This has a twofold purpose. First of all a helmet protects your head. We must allow the knowledge of God's salvation protect our mind. The head is above the entire body. But second of all let the protection of our salvation cover us from head to toe. Let the knowledge of our salvation trickle from the mind and cover the rest of our body.

And finally we must use the sword of the Word of God. We can see an example of this through Christ himself in Matthew 4:1-11. Jesus is in the wilderness and is tempted by Satan three times, and three times Jesus responds by saying, "It is written…" followed by relevant Scripture. In order to know the words to use in these encounters, we must study the sword- the Word of God.

Finally, we are to pray continually. That really is our biggest action in the battle. It is important to make our requests known to God. Pray continually for his strength and power to show up and fight the fight for us.

What I found interesting in studying putting on the armor, and fighting in the spirit is that not once does it tell us that we are to do the fighting. We don't have to do anything but show up prepared and in the armor of God, and then stand firm and fully protected in our armor. That's it. As humans we want the formula or the recipe for success. But we don't have it. It is not by our might, nor by our power. It is not through our words or our anything we do. It is through God's power the battle is won (Zachariah 4:6). He is the one who is greater than our enemy, not us (1John 4:4).

You can see in the Old Testament time and time again where God tells the Israelites to show up, but he tells them that he will fight for them (Exodus 14:14; Deut. 3:22; 2 Chronicles 20:15; 1 Samuel 17:47). This battle, the spiritual battle we are in, is God's battle. He will do the fighting; all we need to do is show up and be obedient.

Even in the story of Michael and Satan, Michael simply said, "The Lord rebuke you." He didn't say, "I rebuke you." He didn't use a lot of words to do it. Just four small words did the trick. Zachariah 3:2 also tells the story of Joshua the high priest standing before God the Father and Satan was standing to his right throwing out accusations. The Lord said to Satan, "The Lord rebuke you."

From both of these examples, there was not a big theatric display of power. There were not a lot of words. All that was necessary was "the Lord rebuke you". I have begun this simple practice in spiritual warfare. Many words are spoken to God, few to my enemy. I pray protection over my family, I plea the blood of the Lamb over my home, I pray for wisdom and discernment, I quote Scripture as Jesus did in the wilderness, and I speak 6 words to my enemy, "The Lord, Yahweh, rebuke you Satan."

Certainly, there are 2 places in Scripture where Jesus speaks about the authority to bind and loosen things on earth and heaven. We have been given certain authority over spiritual matters, but we are to remember that mankind is not the source of that power. It is God's power that keeps spiritual beings in check. Angels and demons actually have more power than we do if we are acting outside of God. Only when we stand under his umbrella of protection does our authority apply. When we enter spiritual warfare outside of God's instruction, without his wisdom and discernment, when we speak our own words, we will have no authority over the demons (Acts 19:13; Matthew 17:20).

Fighting our enemy is tricky. Knowing our enemy is tough. It requires discernment, testing and a right relationship with God. But as Warriors of Christ in this battle, we need to do our best to stay alert and on top of this battle called life. We show up prepared with a yielding heart, and God does the rest.

*(1),(2),(3),(4) Sourced in Back

"Who am I, that the God who sees my sin, would look on me with love and watch me rise again?" ~Casting Crowns

"And even if you do it wrong and miss the joy I planned, no matter what may happen child, I'll never let go of your hand." ~Don Fransisco; I'll Never Let Go of Your Hand

"…and provide for my self again, and supply for my selfish sin. In spite of the knowledge You are a perfect friend…" ~Flame; Devil's Bread

"Welcome to my world and the life that I have made where one day you're a prince, the next day you're a slave." ~Casting Crowns;The Prodigal

Chapter 10
When We Fall In the Dance

Some people say that animals do not think or have emotions, but after owning Phoenix, my German Shepherd, I have to say I disagree. You can see his emotion all over his face and in his behavior. I'm not sure why, but for some reason this dog cannot seem to behave himself. We love him, but he is simply naughty. I don't believe that he wants to do things to get into trouble; I don't even think that he wants to disappoint us. He simply doesn't want to do what he knows he ought to. For example, if we call for him to come, sometimes he will immediately come to us, other times you can almost see him contemplating whether or not he wants to comply, and other times he will straight up turn away.

Both of my dogs greet me at the door when I come home, both bearing gifts. Tanner, my Cocker Spaniel, usually has one of his treasured toys in his mouth, Phoenix who learned this behavior from Tanner will bring me a shoe (he destroys all of his own toys so he rarely has one to bring me). Both prance around proudly with their treasures.

One day when I came home from my morning jog, my Tanner came running at me to greet me as usual, but Phoenix was missing. As I looked across the kitchen I could see his nose peeking out of the doorway to the stairwell into the basement. I called to him, but his nose slowly backed away and disappeared. As I made my way across the kitchen, it became obvious why he had hid from me instead of greeting me. The trashcan was not dumped over, but it was evident he had been rummaging through it by the trash strewn across the kitchen floor.

I continued over to the doorway of the stairwell, but Phoenix had run to the bottom of the stairs and around the corner. I called to him, and he finally appeared ears back and belly to the ground. He would not look at me. I finally got him to come up the stairs and I asked him in a stern voice "What did you do?" He ran in a circle, belly low to the ground. Tanner on the other had continued to jump up and down and prance around with his toy, apparently oblivious to the situation with Phoenix.

I'm not sure if Phoenix's behavior was purely fear driven or if he had a little bit of shame too. Whatever it was, it was certain he was afraid to be in my presence and that fear was connected to his behavior while I was gone.

Don't we behave much the same way? When we have messed up how do we react spiritually? Do we feel the normal confidence to enter the presence of our Holy God? Or do we hide? There have been times in the worship service at church that I am there in body, but spiritually I am checked out. In my shame I want to avoid connecting to God as much as possible. Can you relate? If you can I would like to add this-where we go from there makes all the difference in the world.

There is a perfect parallel in the Bible about two men who blew it and the differences in how they responded. We actually touched on it briefly in the last chapter, but let's take a closer look. Peter and Judas both messed up big time on the very same day, but as we look at their stories they both ended very different. I'd like to take a moment to really dissect these two situations and see what lessons we can glean from them.

During what has been titled the Lord's Supper, Jesus tells the 12 that one will betray him. All of the disciples were astonished and began to question who it may be. I would like to pause here for just a moment. I'm only speculating here, I have nothing other than my own heart to give me reason to wonder this, but I can't help wondering what types of undisclosed thoughts and insecurities resided inside of these men for them to ask that. It seems to me if all were completely steadfast and pure at heart toward Jesus, they wouldn't have to ask if it was them.

Years ago I left my home church for a short time. I left during a season when a split occurred though that was not my reason for leaving. My reason was in part because of hurt feelings and a misunderstanding that happened that I did not properly address. Eventually we addressed the misunderstanding and came back. The church grew to the point we had to add a larger sanctuary. The pastor announced from the pulpit that often times with great growth like our church experienced also comes very real friction, and it was a very real possibility that disruption could happen like before and cause another split and people may leave. Then he said these key words "…and I already know who it may be." The exact words that went through my mind was "surly not me." This story really has little else to do with this chapter other than to call out the human nature within each of us. I do not believe the disciples would have asked that question unless there was something in the each of them to cause them to question.

Back to Peter and Judas.

Judas had already made his plans to betray Christ, he had discussed it with the religious leaders and he was paid 30 pieces of silver. Judas knew exactly who Jesus was speaking of when he said someone would betray him. Immediately he arose from the table to go do what he planned to do. I have heard all kinds of theories about Judas' reasons for betraying Jesus. I have heard that he may have been disappointed that Jesus was not the kind of Messiah he had hoped he would be, and therefore no longer believed he was the Messiah. I have heard that he was trying to force Jesus into an action that he was certain Jesus was going to do. In other words Judas didn't like Jesus' timing so he was trying to "force his hand" so to usher in the new kingdom. I have heard that he was simply greedy and wanted the money. Perhaps it was that he was greedy, wanted the money, and thought Jesus would handle the situation differently than he did. After all, he had seen Jesus do many miracles in the past. He had likely even been present when the people tried to stone or kill Jesus on a couple other occasions; maybe he thought Jesus would get out of it again.

It doesn't really matter why Judas betrayed Jesus; the fact is he did it. It wasn't out of fear or confusion. It was deliberate.

I wonder where he was during the trial that was given to Jesus. Matthew 27 says that as soon as he had heard Jesus was condemned to die he had remorse and gave the money back to the leaders but before he did, he confessed to them all that he had condemned an innocent man. Does that mean he had no idea the plan was to kill Jesus? Maybe he never thought about what was coming after he received his silver. Or maybe he did know the consequences, but he was so caught up in his frame of mind in that moment he didn't care until it was too late.

Can you relate? Have you ever known you were walking down a deadly road but you were so caught up in your mindset that you did not want to turn around? I have. I always hate the end result, but in the moment it's as if I don't care. I wonder if that's is what Scripture means when it says Satan entered him, or did Satan enter Judas in a literal way? Perhaps Judas opened the spiritual doors by what he chose to set his mind on.

I feel like none of this is really relevant when it comes to sin. It is not how or why Judas betrayed Jesus. He may have played a big role in the physical sense that got Jesus on the cross, but in reality I played a big role in why Jesus went to the cross too. It was not what he did, that ought to be our focus, but what he did afterwards that ought to be the focus.

Judas felt remorse, he confessed his sin, but he never sought reconciliation; he hid. In the end Judas takes the cowardly way out by taking his own life. How could the story have been different if Judas had sought out his friends and confessed to them? What would have happened if he had prayed to the Father the way Jesus had taught him to pray? Or what if he had gone out to the site of the crucifixion and tried to seek forgiveness while Jesus was on the cross. Crucifixion was a long drawn out process. He could have tried to seek out Jesus, but instead he hid, and then he committed suicide.

Judas died in his shame and regret. Was he too proud to face his friends? Too afraid that they would be angry and speak truth? Too afraid of facing Jesus? Too afraid to grapple with the choices he made? What ever it was it led to his death, and to spiritual destruction, but it also gives us insight into his heart. Judas walked away from everything good Jesus had to offer him because he messed up and he did not try to make it right.

Peter also betrayed Jesus on that same night, on a different level, but in multiple ways. After Jesus announced someone would betray him and Judas left, another conversation came up. It seems that this discussion happened on their way to the Mount of Olives. Jesus told his disciples that they would all fall away that very night Peter boldly proclaimed he would never fall away, but Jesus informed him that Peter would not only fall away, he would deny even knowing Jesus three times before the rooster crowed in the morning. I believe Peter tried to make good on his promise to die for Jesus later when the soldiers came to get their beloved Messiah.

Before the arrest happened, Jesus asked Peter, James and John into the garden with him. He asked them to pray with him, but they fell asleep. Even after Jesus came back and found them sleeping and again asked them to pray, they continued to sleep. I am sure after Jesus was crucified they thought back to that moment and wondered why they could not stay awake to pray with him. Why wouldn't they take their friends request more seriously. I would imagine they had remorse for their weakness that night.

When the soldiers came for Jesus, I believe Peter thought that was his moment to shine, the moment to prove to Jesus that he was willing to die for him. As he pulled out the sword and swung, he likely thought he was doing a great mighty act for his Lord, but then Jesus reprimanded him. Have you ever put yourself in Peter's shoes at that moment? I think I would feel dejected. I would feel confusion because my Lord had just reprimanded me when I was trying to defend him. My feelings would be so hurt I may not even know what to do with myself.

This is where Peter's story hits a crescendo of mess-ups. Peter followed Jesus and the soldiers from a distance, and then waited outside of the place where Jesus was put on a midnight trial. I'm sure that reprimand was playing back in his mind as he waited outside warming his hands by the fire. He probably didn't even remember the conversation that had taken place with Jesus about how he would deny him in that moment. Peter's world had just been flipped upside down, I'm certain his mind was swirling with questions. In fact, the earlier conversation probably never even came to his mind when he was asked three times if he was a follower of Christ, and out of his fear three times he claimed he had never met Jesus. The third time he even began to curse, so he could get the point across, I suppose. But then the rooster crowed and he looked up and he saw Jesus looking straight at him. Wow, what do you do with all of that mess? What must he have been feeling when he looked into his masters eyes seconds after cursing his name?

I think that Peter's determination to hold steadfast to Jesus was short lived. At first, he was fiery in his resolve, but then he faced confusion and hurt feelings, which led to a loss of all focus. Can you relate to this one at all? Once again, I can. I can't tell you how many times I have proudly proclaimed my allegiance to God no matter what, and then I hit the wall and like a spoiled child I have lost all compass. I get frustrated and mess up even more out of my disappointment and fear.

Both Judas and Peter blew it and they both saw the error of their own choices. They both felt remorse for their behavior. We read about them, and it is easy to feel amazed that they could blow it so hard when they were in the very presence of God. I mean they spent time with him in the flesh. But at a closer glance it is easy to see they are not too far from the rest of us. What really makes the difference is what they do with their mistakes after the fact. Judas hides, but Peter does not.

After the death of Jesus Peter went back to normal life. I would imagine that he spent time in regret; I would bet that he relived the last night of Jesus' life over and over again and he beat himself up for how he handled it. But he went to his friends for support. I wonder if they exchanged stories of regret with each other, after all, they all fell away. Peter was ashamed, but his heart was humble, and repentant.

After Jesus came back to life and came to visit the disciples, Peter did not hide. In John we are told a beautiful story about an interaction between Peter and Jesus. Though we know that Jesus had already appeared to his disciples before this encounter we don't know what Peter's response was to Jesus in the initial visits. What we do know is that Peter had decided to return to his original trade of being a fisherman. He was out doing life the way he had done life before he knew Jesus. The account in John states that in his third appearance to the disciples, Jesus was walking along the shore and he calls out to the men who were fishing with Peter, (which included several other disciples). When they realize it was Jesus, Peter wrapped his outer garment around himself, jumped into the water and goes straight for Jesus. Can you see this with me? Can you see the love and adoration spilling out of Peter, working almost as some invisible force drawing him to Jesus? Peter was longing to be in the vicinity of his best friend.

Of course the other disciples follow him to shore, but they row up in the boat, rather than run through the water. They all sit down to share a meal of fish, and when they are finished eating Jesus asked Peter if he loves him. Peter says, "Yes Lord, you know that I love you." Jesus responds, "Then feed my lambs." The first time Peter may not have thought too much of the question, but then two more times Jesus asks, and two more times Peter answers the same way. Peter was hurt and maybe even offended that Jesus kept asking him. But what is clear to us when we read it is that Jesus was redeeming Peter's denial. Three times Peter denied knowing Jesus, three times Peter confessed his love to Jesus, and then he was given the mission to tell others about Christ.

Just like Judas and Peter we will fall in our dance with Christ. We are human. Sometimes we may only stumble and other times we may fall so hard we bruise our rear ends. When we are humble in heart, and we do not hide, we give Jesus the opportunity to redeem our poor choices. Hiding only leads to our destruction, one way or another.

*(1),(2),(3) Sourced in back

*"Lord, my God, I called to you for help
and you healed me."~Psalm 30:2*

*"The sacrifice pleasing to God is a broken
spirit. God, You will not despise a broken
and humble heart."~Psalm 51:17*

*"I live in a high and holy place, but also with the one
who is contrite and lowly in spirit, to revive the lowly
in spirit and the contrite. I will not accuse forever,
nor will always be angry...I punished them and hid
my face in anger...I have seen their ways but I will
heal them. I will heal them and restore them."
~ Isaiah 57:15-18*

*"Surly the arm of the Lord is not too short to
save, nor his ear too dull to hear."~Isaiah 59:1*

*"Jesus hold me now, I long for your embrace, I beat
and broken down, I can't find my way out. Jesus hold
me now."~Casting Crowns; Jesus hold me now.*

Chapter 11
Dancing Through Healing

"If my people who are called by my name will humble themselves and pray. If they seek my face and turn from their sins, I will hear, I will forgive and I will heal their land."

This is the very foundation for healing. I have known this Scripture for years, I have sung songs about it, yet I did not grasp onto the formula to find healing, not until recently.

This entire book has been written during a process of God healing me. It was not my intention when I started this book for it to be a documentation of my journey, but it was God's intention.

The dance of healing truly combines everything from chapters three through ten.

Let me begin by saying, It is my educated belief that we spend the first 20 years of our lives becoming broken, but it takes a lifetime to heal. Our brains are not fully developed until we are 25 years old. As a result, we have experiences that our minds cannot wrap around. Since we cannot process our experiences with good understanding, we embrace lies about life, family, relationship, and ourselves.

As an individual with a learning disability, a survivor of sexual and emotional abuse, and a strained mother daughter relationship, I embraced many lies about myself. (By the way my mother is my best friend these days, no more strain there). For years my experiences and the lies I embraced as a result of those experiences influenced many poor choices I made in my life.

Seven years ago, I made a bad choice based on some of those lies and that decision put me in a bondage that kept me in toxic patterns. At the time that I made the choice, I had already addressed many of the lies I believed and God had graciously healed me in many ways; but some dangerous residue remained at the core of my being. Not to mention some pretty ugly subconscious rebellion toward God. Instead of addressing it right after my bad choice, I covered over my sin, and I began to build up a beautiful lie. In the meantime I was dying inside. The time finally came where I was ready to admit my mistake, minimally, but only to God, no one else. My pride and my need to be good kept me in bondage.

There were consequences to my choices, but I felt the need to carry those heavy consequences as punishment. To be honest, I believe God gave me those consequences, and allowed me to stay in them for those seven years so that I would learn the lesson, and not forget it. Scripture says that "God disciplines those he loves" (Proverbs 3:12, Hebrews 12:6), and that is exactly what was going on.

Eighteen months ago, I had a conversation that kicked off an incredible, yet necessarily painful journey. I begged God to make me real again. By begging him, I was asking him to come into my situation…into my pain. Soon, I was unpacking a whole lot of hidden baggage. Some of the baggage was from 20 or even 30 years ago. The baggage included disappointments of my childhood, the reality of relationships in my life: past, present, and future. It required recognizing that my choices from 20 years ago were still affecting my children even now. I had to confess those sins and submit them to God. I had to stop blaming others for where I had been hurt and embrace the fact that I was a part of my own toxic patterns. It wasn't just that I was manipulated; it was also that I was a willing participant to be manipulated. It wasn't just that I was abused, I continually offered myself to the abuse. It wasn't just that I was being controlled, I was controlling.

At that point I needed to humble myself and pray. I had to be ready to be vulnerable enough to embrace my very own ugly and ask God to come into it. I had to confess that I was a liar, prideful, controlling and a sinner. I began to ask God to expose my lies, and speak truth into each and every situation that was affected by my choice seven years ago.

Through the process God revealed to me that I have clung to lies that kept me in a victim role, and that victim role was killing me, and my children. I was too proud to see that I was contributing to my own victimization, but I have. I have asked God to bring truth to these areas. What He has done in my life since then has been mind blowing. He has annihilated the lies I believed that have kept me in prison for 35 years.

I share my story to be sure you understand that I know broken, I understand pain, and I understand that there is a certain amount of both that are necessary to heal. Here are the things that I have learned in this process.

#1 Run towards the pain.

Referring back to chapter 3, I talked about being authentic. This is exactly what I mean, by run toward the pain. Where ever the pain is go there, expose it. Ask God in. As I write this, I am in my Human Development class showing my students a movie about PTSD. The professionals are reiterating exactly what I am saying as I write it. Don't pretend it isn't there it only makes it worse. Go there in your mind and emotions. Talk about it with trusted people. Run towards it. Feel it. Whether the pain is embedded in sin, disappointment or heartache; all require healing. Run towards the pain.

#2 Confess all sin, including sinful feelings.

Be as humble as you can when you confess. I recognize that sometimes you may feel justified in your sin. Sometimes when someone stomps on my pride, I will defend myself out of my own pride. But my pride is still sin, even if I feel justified. If that is the case, then confess your pride too. One prayer I used as I prayed is, "God this is where I am, whether it's right or wrong this is how I feel. I don't know what to do with it. But here it is." God will honor your heart's desire to be right even if it isn't right. He knows how to mold your responsive heart to be more like his. It is a spiritual process, but it starts with your confession and honesty about your view of your sin.

In a podcast from Walk in the Word(1), James McDonalds states that the kind of confession that is necessary for true repentance to happen is one that not only admits you are sinning, but agrees with God about that sin. True repentance hurts, it is painful. It is the pain that keeps you from doing it again. If that is not where you are when you confess, ask God to bring you to a humble and contrite heart. Again, only God can bring us to that place of true repentance, but we must be open to the process that He wants to take us through to get us there. Humility and a contrite heart are key to the healing power of true repentance.

#3 Find a group of people you can be transparent with.

Man, this one is hard. Some people have a hard time humbly confessing and being transparent with others, but you must find people you can do this with, who are willing to do the same with you. I have been blessed to have a group of two married couples. They love me dearly, and I love them too. They are not perfect, but they are trustworthy, and godly. There is something about getting your "junk" out in front godly loving people that is healing. Be sure that your group is trustworthy. You are trusting them with very valuable information, what they do with it is important. Trustworthy means they will hold it with the greatest confidentiality, but it also means that they will not use your sin as a weapon against you either.

#4 Specifically ask God to heal you, and specifically ask him to reveal the lies you believe.

Again, in my own process I began to confess to God sins from years ago. Not only did I specifically name them, but also I specifically asked him to come into those areas and redeem the consequences of my poor choices. I believe that I was forgiven years ago, but I had not acknowledged the pain involved in my sin, nor had I asked specifically for healing and redemption. God showed himself faithful. He has come into those little tiny broken places of my life and family and began to restore what has seemed un-mendable.

#5 Be still, quiet, and listen

#6 Be still, quiet and listen

#7 Be still, quiet and listen

#8 Be still, quiet, and listen.

Sometimes you will hear something and wonder if it is God. If it is unclear pray and wait. Where there is peace that is where you are to move, or confess. Test the information coming to you. It may not be what other people think is right, but if it is God, it is right. I remember reading "The Ada's House"(2) series by Cindy Woodsmall.

In it a young Amish man met a homeless Englisher woman and her child. He had compassion on her, and gave up his home for her to live in while he lived in a shack outside. He was shunned for allowing her to come into his life, take over his home, and for the depth of kindness he showed her. They all believed she had bewitched him with her tight jeans, and short cropped shirts. In the end, she came to Christ and joined the Amish community. His kindness to her gave her what she needed.

I know this is about a novel, and I am talking about real life, two very different things (of course they got married and lived happily ever after in the book.) But even in real life, sometimes what others see as the "right thing to do" is not what God is saying. Listen to God, not man. Test what you believe is God, be sure it really is God and not you. If it is, be obedient to the spirit not to man.

#9 Be responsive.

There is a difference between wanting God to fix a situation, and allowing him to fix it. Sometimes when God comes into a situation it requires obedience on your part, sometimes that obedience is painful. It may be killing your pride, or killing your flesh. You may be required to cut off something in your life that feels like it is a part of you. If your heart is truly repentant or soft to God, you will obey him. Face your fears, cut off that part of you that keeps you in bondage bite your tongue until you bite it in two if you must. But you must respond to his healing guidance.

I know of a man who swore he wanted to heal his marriage, but his pride was too alive to bring the healing required for restoration. Instead of beating it down, or even truly repenting of it, he fed it. Every confession of his sin was followed by, "But you should see how bad her pride is…", or "I told her that I was sorry, what more does she want from me." This is not the kind repentance God requires from us`. When God cleans us out it hurts.

I love how all along the way of this book God has put materials in my hands to confirm or speak more depth to the wisdom I find in his Scriptures. This chapter is not an exception. As I write this chapter I am finishing up a Beth Moore study entitled "When Godly People do Ungodly Things."(3) (pg105) Beth confirms that healing always starts with hurting. She starts by telling a story about how her name was changed to "Had" because she was "had by sin." She says,

> *"God wanted to make sure I never act like I haven't been had so he left scars. He kept a set on His own hands and feet and left one on [me]. That's OK. My scars bear the marks of death. Don't let anyone tell you that being had won't kill you. It will. It was meant to. If it doesn't, you've been had for nothing and you will be had again.*
>
> *Christ raises the dead only after they die. Before I was Had, God kept saying, "You are not yet Dead." So instead I was had. Christ let Lazarus lie dead for four days, but not because he was mean. Scripture says he loved Lazarus even though He let illness kill him. Perhaps we all need to know how it feels to be dead for a while. But do we believe we might see the glory of God?"*

Her story is about healing through brokenness caused by sin. How we must feel the full weight of our sin, and grieve it. We must be broken, and contrite before God, completely empty of pride or justification for our behavior. But honestly all areas that cause us great pain, not just the sinful areas, must go through some sort of death if we are to heal through it. Whether it is disappointments, grief, or where our broken childhoods affected us in negative ways, healing will only come with death, but the beauty that comes with the resurrection is amazing. Oh to taste the goodness of God after that kind of death. If only more people were brave enough to let God teach them the dance steps of healing. Child of God, I urge you to let go of your fear, and your sin. Let go of your pride. Let God break you. Let him bring you to the cross. Let death come, so that he may raise you up with joy, and goodness. Let him teach you the dance steps of healing.

*(1),(2),(3) Sourced in back

"For you are saved by grace through faith, and this is not from yourselves; it is God's gift-not from works, so that no one can boast. ~Ephesians 2:8-9

"...Deserving of desertion, servants of destruction, and everyday we taste of a grace that we're unconcerned with. My sin I should be burned with, I'm guilty filthy and stained but he became a curse, drank my cup and took my pain." ~Lecrae; Lucky Ones

Chapter 12
Dancing In His Grace

Grace is somewhat of a complicated concept for me to wrap my mind around. I have tried to avoid writing this chapter because of my inability to understand it at more than a simplistic level. But through the persistence of the Holy Spirit, here I am, writing this chapter. I realized one of the reasons I was having a hard time understanding it, is that there are many different definitions to the word grace. I did a Biblical word search on it and found that it means anything from kindness to something good in appearance, like the grass (What does that even mean?).

But what does it mean to dance in God's grace? Some explain grace by saying it is God's unmerited favor, and though that is absolutely true, I felt like it was not truly encompassing the depth of this concept. I have also heard it said that through God's grace we have the power to change. But that simple answer was not enough for me either. I have recognized things in my life before, confessed it and asked for the grace to change, and the immediate results were little more than gutting through situations armed with a little head knowledge. Eventually I fell again. Somehow the head knowledge was not penetrating deep enough into my heart to make that change. But while writing this book, and trying hard to avoid writing this chapter I have begun to see a newer depth to God's grace and how it is connected to change. Let me see if I can help you understand it so you can apply it to your dance, the same as I have been doing in my own.

There are three variations to the original context of the word we call grace. Two of the meanings don't really apply at all in the context we are speaking of so we won't even bring them up. The other one, charis, is very relevant. Charis is the unmerited grace we talked about. It is kind loving acts bestowed on us by God or others. This also includes God's redemptive mercy on us. This cleared up a lot for me, often we separate grace and mercy, but in reality God's mercy is one aspect of his grace. God also shows us grace by specifically designing pleasure and joy to be a part of our lives. All God given pleasure is a form of God's grace upon us. Every gift given, every moment of joy, is undeserved by us, but given with joy -from our Father in heaven.

Charis also means the kind of grace that is directly opposite of debt, works or law. So when we fall short, there is no debt, works don't count, and falling short of the law means nothing. This is easy to speak about I suppose, but I don't think it is easily lived out. I believe it is much easier to condemn other Christians when they have obviously fallen short in a way they we think they should have known better, than it is for us to accept that God's grace covers their mistake. I think it can be equally easy to carry shame when we ourselves fall hard rather than to believe God's grace covers our mistake whatever it may be.

But how does God's favor then give us the power to change? How is it God's grace that changes me so much? Or gives me strength to go on? What does God given pleasure and gifts have to do with a work being done inside of me? Here is where I struggled so much. How is grace connected to the change that is constantly going on inside of me? This is where I conclude that another frequently used, not well-understood term comes in. I believe it is through a process called Sanctification.

I was unsure exactly how to define spiritual sanctification, so I looked it up. Sanctify is when we set aside a person, or a thing specifically for God's use. It also means to make holy. The word make indicates there is a process to becoming holy. When we accept Christ, we are not automatically holy; we are in the process of being made holy. In order for us to be sanctified, we must go through the process of becoming sanctified.

Further research indicates that sanctification is a proving of oneself. The Vines Concise Dictionary explains it better than I can, so I will let you read it's exact wording:

> *"Proving oneself holy. This proving refers not to an act of judgment against sin but a miraculous act of deliverance."*

My mother added the words "*...From sin.*" Which helped me put it into context. Deliverance is not something we do, but it is something God does (thus grace).

Imagine someone being held captive in a foreign country. They cannot escape on their own, they are dependent on someone else who has the resources to defeat the captors and pull the captive to safety.

In the sanctification process we are gradually being delivered from sin. It is a moment-by-moment separation from our natural tendencies. God is the author and designer of this separation, but we are his willing servants. If we are not willing to do our part, sanctification will not happen, which limits God's grace bestowed on us.

Think again to the captive. If the hero comes in to save, and the captive refuses to get up, or does not want to leave the prison, how will the rescuer be able to deliver him from the prison?

How does God separate us from sin?

The separation process is gradual, but we must be willing to actively pursue God and learn from him. One way he sanctifies us is through reading his Word. Reading his Word alone is not enough, we must also allow it to penetrate our hearts and apply it. God teaches us to be holy (sanctified) through conviction, and from the movement of his spirit. We must want the sanctification process to take place and actively pursue God's heart.

At this point you may be wondering what in the world does this have to do with grace. Let me see if I can bring it around and make it all connect, bear with me here:

God gives us unmerited favor, kindness, joy, and mercy. When we realize how much we don't deserve his grace we are moved to respond to God with love for him. We love him by trying to obey him. We love him by getting to know him, by actively pursuing his heart, which at first is not done well. In our ignorance we fall short often, and yet in his grace, he still smiles on us. Our falls do not go unnoticed or unaddressed though. There are times we need correction. So where God's grace does not fall short of our sin, his discipline does kick in.

Discipline is directly linked to the sanctification process. Believe me, I know all about the role of discipline, and the role it plays in sanctification. I fell a lot in my early dance with Christ. It has only been through discipline and God's truth that I have been changed from the inside out. God does not always discipline us when we fall, and it is not always harsh. Sometimes God begins to direct your heart in the way it should go. He does this with His healing truth. Other times our process requires a deeper work, and in this deep work God will discipline us gently, lovingly and effectively. Sometimes the discipline is quick, other times God allows us to sit in the discomfort of our consequences for years to be sure we learn the lesson.

But here is the beauty of it. During the entire sanctification process God's grace is always there to pick us up. If we have had well-deserved, harsh consequences, it is only to work out the impurity that keeps us from being holy, not to "get back at us" or to "be mean to us". When the process is over God's grace is the healing balm that covers our battered heart.

It is during the healing we feel and appreciate God's grace. But that appreciation perpetuates us further into a sanctified life of holiness. Can you see the connection?

A True Story of Grace and Sanctification

As I was studying up on this subject, my research took me to the book of Ezra. Here we can clearly see the connection, and we can also see how God gives grace in situations that we don't necessarily find deserving of grace. Let me give you a bit of back-story.

After years of rebellion and warning, Israel was destroyed and many of the land's inhabitants were carried off into exile to Babylon. When King Cyrus of Persia came to power he released the Jews. In all they were away from their home for 48 years.

It was by the Grace of God they were finally released. But God had his reasons for allowing the destruction and exile to take place to begin with. Israel had been warned time and time again that their idol worship and rebellion would lead to severe discipline, yet they continued in their sin. God still loved them, even in their rebellion but he loved them too much to let them continue in their sin against him. The love that was still there is an example of God's grace. The patience God had as they were rebelling is also God's grace.

The exile was a part of God's sanctifying plan for his people. While they were in exile, they missed their homeland, and their traditions. They longed to be reunited with the land God gave them and with the traditions practiced while serving God. In their pain from being exiled, their hearts yearned for God and yearned to be home. By God's grace there was an end to the season of discipline. And they were finally released to go back to their homeland. By the way, God gave them this un-earned favor knowing ahead of time that it would not be long before Israel would fall back into old patterns of doing their own thing.

Israel celebrated as much as a nation free to return to their roots and rebuild possibly could. They immediately celebrated the Passover meal, a celebration that had not taken place in at least 48 years. Some of the offspring had never even had the chance to celebrate this festive time of remembrance.

The nation of Israel was so thankful to be home, celebrating their heritage. They were in a season of "honeymoon" with God. But soon after the celebration Ezra was given the disappointing news that members of Israel's community had married women from neighboring nations. These were people God had specifically told them not to be involved with because of their detestable practices and idol worship.

When Ezra found out he fell to his knees and cried out to God in front of all who could see him. He begged for forgiveness and prayed for God's mercy on Israel. The people were convicted and moved to do the same. With truly repentant hearts the men of Israel confessed their sin, and made things right by sending the foreign women back to their homelands.

God had mercy on them for their sin of marriage to foreign women. Mercy is grace. The situation was one that was difficult as there was a double sin here. These men married women they were commanded not to marry, but then to make it right they had to divorce them. Divorce is also falling short of God's command. God's grace covered both of these areas that were blemished by sin.

As far as I read there were no consequences to their sin this time. My thoughts behind it was that their hearts truly felt remorse, they slipped and fell but the exile was a discipline they remembered. They knew rebellion could lead to another exile, or other consequences that were unfavorable for them. They wanted to please God so when they were confronted with where they had once again fallen short their response to repentance was quick and genuine, leading once again to God's beautiful grace. His response was set in contrast to debt, works, or the law.

Grace for Each Other

I have experienced God's grace in action. I have been strong enough to offer God's grace to others. I have experienced the lack of God's grace from other humans. Amongst the worst offenders have been in the Christian community. Sometimes the more "godly" they are, the less grace they have to offer. I myself have had little grace to offer at times. I wrote a short story, it's a 2 part. The first is where I had experienced a lack of grace from the Christian community, judgment calls on my heart that others didn't have the right to make.

The second part is where I found myself in a situation giving another person no grace for making some of the exact same choices I myself had made. The difference? I was too far removed from the days I behaved that way to give her the same kind of grace that I had longed for from God's people when I was in my sin. The moment I realized I was doing it, I stopped and wrote a repentant short story about it. I will share both parts with you:

The Walk of Shame
Found in John 8:1-11

She had lived most of her life in shame. She never fit in as a child, though she tried. Eventually she learned how to get attention from men, the wrong kind of attention. Her efforts just resulted in rumors, dirty looks and an emptiness that went to the deepest part of her soul. She felt worthless and trapped; and yet, with every new man she had hope. Hope that this time she had found her hero. Hope that this was the lover who would be the one to defend her and save her from the world around her; the love that would stick up for her and free her from the bondage that she felt. But every new relationship ended the same, in disappointment, and her heart being broken once again.

It was while she was with one of these men that she came face to face with Him for the first time. It was an unusually hot day. When she awoke that morning she had the familiar longing in the depths of her soul, so she decided to hide in the embrace of her forbidden lover. She was in his bed when a crowd of her accusers came barging in, ripped her from her lovers' arms, dragged her into the street and threw her down at the feet of Jesus. There was no question they anticipated his judgment upon her. The saddest thing is that each accuser was guilty of committing the same types of sins as she had been committing, but they were better at hiding their transgressions than she was.

As they threw her down they called her names, and mocked her. Even her lover from whose arms she was ripped joined in the accusations. She just lay there on the ground, emotionally bleeding. The horrendous scene being played out that day was confirming every condemnation she felt toward herself. As the emotional assassination continued, she waited for His judgment. But something strange happened instead. He knelt down beside her and looked into her eyes. Suddenly she felt light break through her darkened soul and an unusual peace settled over her. It went into every crevice of her soul. And a new kind of hope came to life inside of her.

As the crowd again began to cry out for her judgment, Jesus stood and said, "Let he who is without sin cast the first stone."

As that realization came to into focus, the insults and condemnation began to fade until there was only a peaceful silence. She kept her face toward the ground for a long moment, afraid to look up. Afraid of what she might see. Cautiously she raised her eyes and her gaze met his. Jesus asked her if there was anyone left to condemn her. "No one sir" she responded.

"Then neither do I condemn you. Go and sin no more (John 8:11; Romans 8:1). Realize you are fearfully and wonderfully made (Ps 139:14). Your sins were many, but they have been washed away. You are a new creation; old things are passed away (2 Cor 5:17). Some people may try to make you feel worthless, but I find you priceless. You are beautiful to me. I love you so much I came to you so I could clean you up, heal you and prepare you to spend eternity with me (John 3:16-17). Follow me and you will never be the same. It's not too late. You are not tarnished goods. YOU ARE BEAUTIFUL (Is.61: 3)."

From the moment she looked into His eyes she was never the same. People still said things for a while. But she knew Jesus thought she was beautiful. She no longer put her security in men (Psalm146: 3-4). She no longer waited for a hero because Jesus, her hero had come, and she will never be the same.

You may think that this is the story of the woman caught in adultery in John 8:3-11, but it's really my story... and it's your story. It's anyone's story who has come to Christ. Perhaps it isn't adultery you were guilty of. Perhaps it wasn't the love of a man you were seeking out to make you whole. That is just the metaphor for what really brought you to the feet of Jesus. We all have our stories of shame, or heartbreak. None of us are alone in our need for a savior to cleanse and heal us. We all have sinned and fallen short of the glory of God. If Christ himself doesn't condemn us, we need to not fear condemnation from others, but instead we need to begin living as children of the King (2 Cor 5:17, Gal 3:26).

All it takes is a moment looking into the face of Jesus to change your life forever. Changed hearts make changed lives. Be still; look into the face of Jesus. Let him change you.

MORE Walking in Shame

…But wait, there's more.

One day I was in town minding my own business when I heard an angry crowd. I turned to looked and saw a familiar scene, only this time I was not in the middle of it. I was on the outside observing. They dragged a woman out into the street and began to stone her. I knew of this woman, I knew what she had done. I kept my distance, I didn't want to get involved, and yet I found myself justifying what this crowd was doing to her.

"After all," I thought to myself, "this woman had been caught doing something worse than I ever did. First she left her wonderful husband and her children for another man. But then she got tired of that man and began cheating on him with another man. Neither guys knew it but she was sleeping with them both. She just got caught in the bed of the new boyfriend, and she's now been dragged out in front of the whole town naked and exposed. Everyone's ridiculing her and calling her a whore, because well, that's what she is, right? A woman who jumps from one man's bed to another's is a whore and we can all see she has earned that title. I personally don't want to say too much because I was caught in adultery once, but my sin was much different than hers.

Besides, most of us learn from our mistakes, don't we? She left her first husband, and shortly after that she realized she was a fool, but then she did the same foolish thing. Now here she is in front of this angry mob getting exactly as she deserves. I won't stone her like the others are; I'll just watch the girl get exactly what was coming to her. What kind of woman sleeps around like that anyway...?"

Suddenly I looked over at my uplifted hand...wait a minute what am I holding? Is that a stone in my hand? How many have I thrown? I looked over at her lying in the middle of the accusing crowd. She was hurting, and humiliated...exposed. It seemed like every stone thrown fed the frenzy of destroying this woman's soul. Slowly I began to see her turn into a reflection of me.

...Who have I become? I hated the stones being thrown at me, why was I throwing stones at someone else? I dropped my stone and walked over to her. I couldn't stop the crowd from throwing stones at her, but perhaps I could protect her. I called out to Jesus, the one who saved my life. If she knew Him, maybe she would change the way she lives. If He were here He would know how to change the situation of condemnation for her the way He did for me. Instead of continuing to join them in condemning her, I began to pray for her.

How quickly we forget where we were when God changed us.

God has grace on us all the time. No matter what horrible, embarrassing, sinful, ugly choices we make. His grace at minimum is forgiveness of those sins. His grace may not extend to the point of no consequences all the time, but sometimes it does. God knows when it is best to extend that kind of grace (mercy) and when it is best not to. But the forgiveness is always there.

God is wise and he sees beyond our human behavior straight down to the life experiences each individual has had which fuels their behavior. He knows that subconsciously we hold lies that perpetuate sinful choices. Sanctification is the process where God removes those lies to make us holy and set apart. He knows how to do that. Some lies are removed easily; a simple word of truth is all that is required to remove them. Others require a long painful process. God knows the lies held behind a person's ugly behavior, we do not. It is not up to us to cast stones. God knows the lies we hold behind our own behavior; we often don't even see our behavior as ugly. We are equally vulnerable to have stones thrown at us. It's best to keep the stones on the ground, and pray for one another, better yet, come along side and hear each other's stories and be a support to one another during tough times.

As I write, I am reminded of a story Max Lucado told in his book "In the Grip of Grace"*(1), if the goal to reach redemption is to jump as high as the moon, does it matter if you jump 14 inches off the ground and another only 6? You're both way off, and in the grand scheme of things, your extra 8 inches makes no difference.

Honoring God's Gift of Grace

There are many people who accept God's grace, but they do not seem to grasp the magnitude of it. They accept it, but continue in their sin with the attitude "God will forgive me." Let me clarify, at times we are caught up in a sin so deep we cannot seem to pull out of it.

When I first came to Christ with a surrendered, authentic dedication, I was caught up in a sin that was too big for me to walk out of. I knew I needed to change, but I was unable to just pull myself together and walk away. I spent the next year and a half on my knees crying out to God for help. My heart broke at my own spiritual stains. God showed me grace during that time. He whispered truth to my battered heart. He began to heal places in my soul that only he could reach. I continued in the lifestyle I was caught up in, but he healed my foundation. I did not passively ask God to fix me; I pursued him and was obedient where I was strong enough to be. I read his word frequently, I went to church consistently, and I was steadfast in my tithe. God showed me grace. I changed what I could change, and left what I couldn't for him to change. He did.

His truth changed me until the day came where he clearly required a big painful step. It was painful, perhaps one of the most painful decisions of my life. But I was given the choice between God, or an idol. I chose God and I had to leave the idol and the outcome in God's hands. I have not always left it in his hands; I've not been perfect in my faith about the situation I walked away from. But over the years God has worked on deeper things connected to that situation and through his grace and his sanctification process I can see beauty. If you are in a similar situation, rest assured you are not taking advantage of God's grace. Keep your face to the floor, keep confessing and let God discipline you and sanctify you.

On the other hand, if you have an attitude that you may indulge in behavior that you know grieves God; that is different. In Romans 6:1-2 Paul asks the question, "What shall we say then? Shall we go on sinning so that grace may increase? By no means..." Here is the gist of it though, If you are truly repentant towards God, if you truly long to experience his grace, if you truly love him, you don't want to take advantage of his kindness towards you.

A man was married to a woman. He loved her intensely. It was not that she had done anything to earn his love. She did not come from prestige; she did not hold much beauty. He saw that she was morally lost and had little understanding of real love. He longed for her. He loved her intensely. He didn't need a flawless love in return from her; he simply wanted to have the chance to love her.

After years of pursuing her she finally gave herself to him in marriage, but never in heart. Day after day she would visit other lovers from her past. He would ask her to stop, but she did not. Day after day, year after year she committed adultery on him. She would apologize knowing he accepted her apology. She knew it might hurt him, but she wanted to be with her old lovers. It was more important to her to hold onto those things that she loved than to love the one who loved her so much. Besides, she knew he forgave her, so why should she have to go without?

Does that sound like love to you? Does she seem committed to him at all? How appreciative is she for his undeserved love towards her? How appreciative is she of his continual grace and mercy at her adulterous affairs? If you are a Christian you are the bride of Christ. If you feel like you are doing good enough with God, but you are not willing to give up behaviors you know are hurting God, then you are this wife. If your heart truly accepted his grace, and you are crushed when you hurt him, then you would never justify your behavior and hold onto it.

Love does not take advantage of God's grace. Love's heart breaks when we break the heart of our beloved. Being under Gods' grace means we don't earn it, for it is unmerited, but it also does not treat it like dirty rags tossed in the corner either. We hold that grace high, and we hold the one who gave it to us even higher. Truly embracing grace means that we show our appreciation by acting out of love toward God. Really understanding grace means we are suddenly moved to seek how we may now bless his heart.

*(1) Sourced in back

> *"Dear God, if today I lose my hope, please remind me that your plans are better than my dreams." ~unknown*
>
> *"Though He slay me, I will hope in him; yet I will argue my ways to His face." ~Job 13:15*
>
> *"And so, Lord, where do I put my hope? My only hope is in you." ~Psalm 39:7*
>
> *"Never be afraid to trust an unknown future to a known God." ~Corey Ten Boom*

Chapter 13
Dancing the Dance of Hope

What exactly is Hope?

Go to any Christian bookstore or gift shop and you will likely see wall decorations, little trinkets, and stationary with the word Hope scrolled across it. We use this word for encouragement. It is one of those beautiful concepts we depend upon in our society. It goes along with well-being, peace, grace, mercy; all words of optimism right? Well, not really. Not when you stop to really think about what hope means. Romans 8:22-25 tells us how it feels to hope and my experience is that Paul was right on when he wrote:

> *We know that the whole creation has been groaning as in the pains of childbirth right up to the present time. Not only so, but we ourselves who have the first fruits of the Spirit groan inwardly as we wait eagerly for our adoption as sons, the redemption of our bodies. For in this hope we were saved.* (HERE IT IS) *For hope that*

is seen is no hope at all. Who hopes for what he already has? But if we wait for what we do not have we wait patiently.

That is hope. Waiting patiently for what we do not see. This verse focuses exclusively on the hope of the Spirit, but hope can be about far more than our hope in Christ. We can hope to see a dream fulfilled too. Paul says it's an inward groaning. Isn't that how hope feels; the waiting, the yearning. Hope is painful, but hopelessness is even more painful.

Proverbs 13:12 says, "Hope deferred makes the heart sick."

What are we to do with that? I have to tell you I don't really know. I believe it has something to do with not holding on too tightly to the hopes we have that are not Christ himself. The only hope that is true hope is the hope we have in his promises. Hope in the tiny details of how we get there is false hope. Where there is hopelessness, and I don't mean in the small stuff like "I hope we go on vacation some day" but the bigger things like, "my marriage feels hopeless and I am dying bound to this person even as I try to make the best of it." In those areas simply ask Jesus into the middle of it. It sounds silly I suppose, but perhaps there are lessons that you need to learn before he shows up. And by all means, know the difference between putting your hope in him and putting your hope in your marriage or in your spouse.

In the study "Hope an Anchor for Life." Dr. David Jeremiah recalls a story written by Alfred Hitchcock about a woman who was sentenced to prison for the rest of her life. She made friends with the mortician, and was able to strike up a deal with him. The next person to die she would sneak into the coffin and he would bury her with the corpse, then later that evening the mortician would come back and let her out and she would be free. Her hope was set in the mortician keeping his deal. So the next time there was a death she waited patiently for just the right opportunity to crawl into the casket with no one looking. But once buried she waited and waited to no avail. Eventually she struck a match only to realize she was now buried with the mortician who was supposed to come rescue her. Her hope was dead, and so would she be soon. We must be careful about what and whom we put our hope in.(1)

How to Dance with Hope

In a world full of so much pain, so much unfairness, and so many broken dreams how do we dance the dance of Hope? I wish I had an easy answer. But to be honest, I have to say hope is a hard dance to maneuver. There are times I am steadfast in my hope, there are times I am fearful in it, and there are times that I fight God for control of those things I hope for. In times like that I always end up on my knees crying out for his strength and sometimes for the acceptance that the thing I hope for will never come to pass. But, don't miss that there is beauty in the dance of hope too. It requires courage, the kind of courage most people do not have the "guts" to have.

Something God is beginning to teach me about hope is that he is the only thing we can fully put our hope in, everything else will let us down. Scripture also points to this over and over again. The only hope God truly guarantees is in him, his goodness, and his promises. We may have hopes for other details in our lives, but those hopes may never come to fruition. Our hope must lie in resting in the arms of Christ that if what we hope for does not happen, it is for good reasons that we don't yet understand.

As I began to write this chapter something tragic happened in my life, something that turned my life upside down. It involved a subject of my hopes. At the same time there was another hope, a dream of mine, on the horizon. That dream is now on hold for at least a season, but to be honest it may never come full circle. Because of the situation I am currently in, my perspective on hope has changed immensely. I am now beginning to understand my former beliefs about hope were wrong. In fact, they were more about control than hope. I believe that God wanted to remake my entire perspective on hope so I can teach about it well. But in order to do that he had to first shatter my flawed understanding.

I have realized that sometimes our hopes, even the ones that have the best intentions, are hopes that are fully steeped in self-absorption and self-protection, not in the beauty we think they are. I now recognize that we need to test, and question our motives in some of the things we hope for.

See, the ministry I had longed to establish is a good thing to hope for. But as I'm dancing this dance it is difficult sometimes to know what steps are God's and which ones are my own desires talking. There are Scriptures that offer encouragement. I can cling to them with unrelenting determination, but God will not bless a demanding, or a controlling motive. It doesn't matter how many times I pray and meditate over Hebrews 11, or speak to the mountains that are in the way, or Ask, Seek, Knock; if my motives are about getting my way, or if I have a hidden attitude that believes I have earned it, God will not bless my dreams.

I have realized that at the core of my hope for the ministry, and the core of my hope to someday be published is still the insecure little girl inside of me begging God to use me in order that he may show those who rejected me that I am of value. Those questions that are at the depth of my soul are not questions a ministry is meant to answer. They are questions only God can answer, and only a willing, yielding spirit can receive those answers.

I have realized at the core of my other tragedy is a desire to control. I want control over my pain. Control over my loss. But truly God knows what is best for all involved. Things don't make sense to me, in this situation but God is helping me realize it is not about my plans, or my hopes. Ultimately life is about the kingdom and what lies beyond this life for me and for all of those involved. Whether my hearts desire is ever eased or ever met, the pain in my heart...the groaning is mine to bear until God takes it or fulfills it. I must not cling to hope out of the need to control my life or my pain.

As I'm writing this, I realize the situation I am in is not the first time I have recognized the idea of false hope "In the name of God". I have heard many people speak about the importance of praying over your children, and trusting God with them. I have heard that I should cling unrelenting to the promises in the Bible about how your children will grow to love the Lord when we train them the right way, and trust God with them. An easy example of these "Biblical promises" would be Proverbs 22:6 "Train up a child in the way he should go and when he is old he will not depart from it."

I have to admit, I am walking through the teenage years with my children right now, and my children are not necessarily ascribing to the choices and beliefs I would like for them to choose. I have had multiple well meaning people tell me to cling to the promises and believe God will bring them back. Hope. But then I look at King David, a man after God's own heart. He loved God, and in fact wrote most of the Psalms, yet his son Absalom tried to kill him. Scarier yet is that Absalom died in his rebellion toward God and toward King David.

King David is not the only man of God to lose his children to the enemy. 1 Samuel talks about a man named Eli who loved the Lord, but his children did not walk in God's ways. They turned aside went for dishonest gain, accepted bribes and perverted justice. What am I supposed to do with that in light of holding on to hope that my children will come to share my values?

There is the danger in recognizing the difference between true hope and a false version of hope. Those "hopes" we cling to, the ones that are self-centered, when they do not work the way we want them to can lead to utter confusion. In those moments of defeat, you may have the sense your life is spinning out of control. Unfulfilled hope can also lead to anger. How dare life not bow down and fulfill every dream I have? If we are honest with ourselves we may have to admit to feeling resentment at God when these hopes collapse from under our feet, or at lest I do. Hope can be a difficult thing to navigate through.

This doesn't mean it isn't ok to hope for things other than Christ. It is ok to hope to get the promotion, to hope someday you will find a spouse, hope that the loved one you are praying for will change, hope that the ministry you long to start receives God's blessing and takes off. But, the question to ask is: Where is your security? Are you looking to this hopeful dream to answer questions that lie at the depths of your soul? It can't. Are you trusting God to bring about his will in his time? Or are looking to control certain aspects of this thing you are hoping for? We must learn to hold to our hope gently, as though holding onto a baby chick, not squeezing, or suffocating, but instead holding it loosely so if it jumps away it will not be damaged in the process. The only hope to cling to is our hope in Jesus Christ, because that is the only hope guaranteed in this life.

Don't Rush God

We can learn a few lessons from Abraham about hope. Granted, his story is a little different than ours ever will be. I have wrestled with the fairness of this difference on multiple occasions. See, an angel of the Lord came to Abraham and told him he would receive those things he hoped for. He told Abraham leave your homeland and go to a place I will take you. Out of faith and hope for the fulfillment of the promise Abraham obeyed. Then the angel promised he would make him the father of many nations. He took him to the land of Canaan and made a promise that someday it would be the land of Abrahams heirs. Abraham believed God that all of these things would happen. The problem I sometime have with God (so arrogant isn't it?) is that today we don't have angels telling us our promises. We have certain promises written in God's in-errant Word. But I have never had an angel come to me to give me specifics. If I had, I think it would be easier to know what exactly to hope for, and what to be cautious about. Because we don't have angelic appearances the dance of hope is tricky.

God told Abraham specific things to hope for, and Abraham believed and held tight to that hope, but we can glean another lesson from his story. We must always wait on God's timing to deliver what we are hoping for. God promised Abraham that he would be the father of many nations. Abraham asked God how he would pull it off since he had no children and he was already 75 years old. God responded by telling Abraham specifically that he would open the womb of Abraham's wife, Sarah.

I would imagine Abraham went straight home to Sarah to make a little romance. I can also put my self in his shoes when month after month he felt disappointment as no signs of a pregnancy appeared. Abraham still had the courage to believe that God's promises were true. He still had courage to put his trust in the one true God. But that is where his courage ended.

Here is where Abraham's faith and courage turned into a need for control. After years of trying to get pregnant, Sarah approached Abraham and said, "Maybe God meant for the promise to be fulfilled a different way. I will give you my maidservant. Maybe this is the way the child is meant to be conceived, after all, I'm not getting any younger and either are you." Abraham agreed.

It wasn't long before Hagar was carrying Abraham's child. But, this was not God's plan at all, God was specific that in his timing he would open Sarah's womb, not Hagar's. Abraham did not wait on God to fulfill that yearning, the groaning of hope he felt. He rushed it and took matters into his own hands.

There were consequences to Abraham's impatience. Hagar became bitter towards Sara, Sara resented Hagar, and a child who caused controversy was born. We won't even get into the depth of the mess that Abraham's impatience caused, but to make a long story short Ishmael's decedents are the roots to Islam, the same way Isaac's decedents are the roots to Christianity. To this very day there are tensions between the 2 religious beliefs. You can study up more on that history if you care to know the truth about it, but the final point is this;

the tension there is a toxic consequence to Abraham trying to help God fulfill his promise.

When God does make a promise and when he is the real author of whatever hope we hold dear to us, we must wait on him to bring it to fruition. Anything short of total submission and obedience will only bring us the consequences of heartache.

I have struggled at times with questions about where I may have stepped outside of God's will. There is a hope I hold dear to my heart. Years ago I felt that God whispered a promise about a great longing I have. To this very day I wonder if the "promise" was a result of my own mind, if maybe my longing was so intense that my own inner voice spoke to my heart and promised me something it cannot fulfill. Maybe it was the enemy of my soul whispering a distraction to me, a distraction that could have potential to harden my heart to God when it never came to be. Or is it truly that God whispered a promise to me. It has been 9 years and I still don't know. I have no confirmation about the source of that promise.

If God whispered the promise to me, I can tell you I stepped out of his timing. Out of the ache and to ease my own pain I have made choices that now block this hope from coming into reality for the time being. But the story of Abraham speaks to that. See, God has reassured me that we cannot mess him up. If he made a promise, he can and will fulfill it. And if he didn't make that promise, it is because he sees the full picture. Psalm 139:16 says:

> "...All the days ordained for me were written in your book before one came to be."

This means God does not make promises he knows you will get in the way of fulfilling. He knew before he made the promise to your heart you would make choices to get in the way. He also knows his way around your missteps. There are times to "shelve" our hopes, and just cling to the only hope we can claim for certain. God is in control when we yield to him. But our hope always must be in him, not in the subject of our hopes (Psalm 39:7-8).

Abraham went outside of God's will. He made choices and had consequences; God still gave him the son promised to him; but it happened in God's timing. If God made a promise in your heart, he still can and will fulfill it. You must let go of your control over it though. You do not get to tell God when and how you get your promise fulfilled. Wait on him if you don't want a mess.

Hope Defined

Here is what I am learning about hope, as humans we need it to survive. Living without hope is suffocating and painful. More painful than the groaning we feel as we wait for the fulfillment of hope. Hope gives us freedom to dream. I am writing this portion of the chapter on the other side of my tragedy. So much has happened and changed since that day almost one year ago. I did not realize it at the time, but for years I have lived with very little hope in one area of my life. It felt like a prison. I was suffocating and in a lot of emotional and spiritual pain. I have friends who have told me that I looked and acted like a walking dead. Since then my hopelessness has broken open and I have had an awakening. Hope has gushed back into my soul and I feel alive and free. What I hope for is not promised to come to fruition, but I now have the ability to hope that someday it can, but not in my doing only by the Spirit of God. My hands are off and will remain off the object of my hope.

I have been confused about hope for over a year. I have heard many people say that we use the word hope wrong. That hope is only appropriate to use if it is a sure thing. Anything else is a wish. But the only thing that we are allowed to really call hope then is the hope of our salvation in Jesus Christ. If hope is only in sure things then I cannot say that I have hope that God will bring a friend of mine to Christ because it's not a sure thing. I cannot say that I have hope that God will answer anything specific that I pray for whether it is a job, healing, or a happy marriage. Sometimes he says "no" to my requests, no matter how good my intentions are behind the request. I cannot have hope in my prayers if I take hope the way some say that I must take it. I can only say I wish God would answer my prayers the way I want him to.

So according to this definition, it is never hope when someone I love has been diagnosed with cancer and I pray asking for healing. It is not hope to believe there is a chance their life will be saved. It is only hope to know that God can hear my prayer.

I looked up the word hope to help me better understand what other people were saying about hope, here is what I found:

Hope is:
A feeling of expectation and desire for a certain thing to happen.
To want something to happen or be the case
A feeling of trust

Here is my conclusion. I disagree that it is only appropriate to use the word hope if it is something guaranteed. If it was, then we could never dream without it being simply a wish. It would be wrong to say that it was unrelenting hope that cured someone's cancer. Hope keeps us from getting hard in spirit. It does hurt to long for something whether it is promised or not. I think it is easier to hope for what we know is a sure thing.

Hope also does something beautiful to an individual's soul. It is like life. Without having expectations or desires life becomes bland and the soul becomes numb. That ache of hope somehow brings life. And when hope is deferred it makes the heartsick and is like a crushing of the bones. Which can make it easy to stop hoping for the unsure things out of self-protection.

Self-protection is an ugly deadening thing. Cessation of hope comes from fear. Fear is fueled by the question "What if…"

What if I'm wrong?
What if this ends in disappointment?
What if this is not God, but only in my head
What if I am laughed at?
What if…

Staying soft enough to hope, realizes "Sometimes I am wrong, disappointed, sometimes it's not God, sometimes I am laughed at, or rejected.

Still I dare to hope."

Please, please, always hope, but always hold your hope loosely, and be ready to let go if God says no.

One last thing on the meaning of hope; notice the last definition. That is why I think so many people have said we can only hope for what we are sure will happen. The definition says hope is a feeling of trust. This definition is different from the prior two and comes from the way the word was used in ancient Greek days, during the time of the Bible. Hope is trust. This goes back to holding onto hope loosely. See it is not in the relationship I put my trust in; it is not the job I put my trust in. I may hope they happen, but I must recognize my saving grace is Christ himself, and nothing else. Not a person, relationship, or job. All other things must be held loosely and if I cling to them I am clinging to the wrong thing. I will soon be buried 6 feet under with the death I have put all of my hope in. With Christ I have hopes that the impossible is possible, but I must be willing to accept that the impossible may or may not be God's will for my life.

Take a moment to think about these things.

What are your hopes and dreams?

Who or what are you placing your hope (or the fulfillment of your hopes) in?

Is your hope more about control or is it genuine hope?

Have you become self-protecting and as a result quit hoping for things?

*(1) Sourced in back

"The best way to get along with others is to not expect them to be like you."~Joyce Meyers

"And He personally gave some to be apostles, some to be prohets, some evangelists, some pastors and teachers, for the training of the saints in the ministry, to build up the body of Christ." Ephesians 4:11-12

"...because you are still fleshy, For since there is envy and strife among you, are you not fleshy and living like unbelievers?" 1 Corinthians 3:3

Chapter 14
Dancing Puzzle Pieces

The day the concept that God's people are like puzzle pieces came to me in the middle of a church service. I was visiting some friends at the church they regularly attend. It was very different from the way my church does worship. I found myself becoming agitated at the way the people in this service behaved. I have to admit that even in the moment I didn't agree with my own judgment that I kept passing on these people, but I couldn't seem to help myself. See, I like a quiet reflective worship time. I want to be lost in thought and in reflection on Christ. Sometimes I close my eyes and imagine heaven, and I see myself on my knees before the throne of God in worship, sometimes I get lost in my own prayer rather than singing. In this service it was never going to happen, the people were too noisy. It was like a pep rally, they kept telling me to jump up and down, they told me to clap and hoot and shout to God. As an individual who has studied psychology, my mind began to analyze their tactic and I believed they were attempting to create religious experience by encouraging some version of mass hysteria. If I am shouting out to God because someone else told me to, or because everyone else is, then it is not genuine worship. Right?

But what kept coming to my heart is that I don't know what their experience is. Perhaps what they feel is real. Maybe they feel an overwhelming movement inside of them that demands a release of shouting to the Lord. Perhaps if they were in a church service where they were being encouraged to quietly reflect and pray during worship they would be bored out of their minds, yawning and unable to worship. Knowing personality types, I suppose a theory that concludes people genuinely worship different even makes sense. Extraverts are loud and feel energized by exterior experience, introverts like internal experiences. I'm a rather extreme introvert. I was so stuck on my own way of worship that I was annoyed and judgmental of other genuine versions of worship.

My visit to that church got me thinking further about many angles of the differences within the body of Christ. What if sometimes we get so stuck on our version of God, worship, study, interpretation of Scripture, and so forth that we miss out on what God is trying to reveal to us through another person? Maybe it would be wise not to be too quick to shut other opinions out. Certainly we need to be cautious about it. There are teachers out there that are teaching things that go directly against God's word. It is never a good idea to grasp hold of a teaching that says there is no hell, that homosexual marriage is a good idea, or that God wants us to be happy. But maybe God has given you one perspective of his character and another person a different perspective that also lines up with Scripture. Perhaps God is gifting both in different understandings, and we need to see how it lines up rather than argue about who is right or wrong.

Let me clarify a little. God has given me an amazing ability to love and show mercy. I can "walk a mile in someone's shoes" fairly easy. This is a gift from God. I can also speak the truth in love very gently, almost too gently. In fact sometimes so gently that the person I am speaking to may think that I condone behavior that I really do not. I certainly need to get better at speaking directly, though over the last few years I have improved a little.

I know of other individuals who can speak boldly the truth of God, and even speak loudly that God's love is not just about mercy, but also about judgment and justice. Sometimes these people speak with great penetrating words and convict perfectly. Other times they speak out of line and cause a great deal of damage. I believe that both the gift of speaking in love, being gentle, and accepting others in mercy as well as the gift of speaking the truth about God's judgment are Biblical. Both mercy and judgment happen in the Bible, but an extreme of either is harmful.

I am not wrong for showing mercy when mercy is not deserved, however it is wise to remember there is a time and a place to speak difficult truth boldly. It is not merciful at all if I am not speaking bold truth when it is appropriate. Those of us who are gifted in mercy must also remember that there is a time and place to warn people about judgment. A murderer should not be shown mercy to the extent of freedom from any consequence of his actions. Just because his neurological pathways were damaged as a result of the horrible child abuse he experienced in his childhood does not excuse his behavior. Yet sometimes that's how deep my mercy can go. This crosses over the line of mercy into enabling unrepentant sin.

My ability to show mercy has amazed some people, and at the same time made them cringe. How could I love someone who has been so evil? Mercy is where God has gifted me; it comes natural.

On the other hand, I have watched as others can commence speaking bold truth beautifully. Truth that I feel I could never speak tactfully. They can pull it off in a way that heals and changes lives. However, these same people may also speak truth in ways that come off assaulting. When someone constantly tries to entrap others into a debate about right and wrong, or constantly talk about God's judgment they turn others off. I have actually experienced some people who seem like they get excited at the thought of God's judgment on others. This is harmful to people who are looking into the lives of these Christians, especially if they don't know Christ yet.

When anyone takes the stance that "truth is truth and I will not sugar coat it." They risk doing more harm to the kingdom of God than good. Truth may be truth, and it needs to be heard and understood, but there is a time and place to speak it. It is never an effective tactic to walk up to a homosexual and tell them, "You are going to go to hell if you do not stop this behavior and repent." If they do not first get the chance to experience and understand God's love for them, they will never be moved to repent. Instead, they will be made to feel like you are pushing an angry vengeful God on them. Why would anyone want to serve that God?

As you can see, on their own, these two "gifting's" from God, or truth revealed could go bad. There is a beautiful balance between the two. But far too often the mercy filled person becomes angry at the "bold truth speaker's" words and the "bold truth speaker" criticizes the "mercy giver". We are puzzle pieces. God has a big picture, and that big picture requires several pieces to come together in unity for that picture to be complete. But instead what tends to happen is we get puffed up in the part of the picture God is revealing to us, and we get angry with people who are having a different part of the puzzle revealed to them, when God intends for us to come together and learn from each other to get the whole. When we shut those other puzzle pieces out we are in danger of going to an extreme.

If you are anything like me you have heard the Scriptures that talk about working as the body of Christ, and you understand it to an extent. I have been guilty in the past of hearing the Scripture and thinking to myself "I get this, we are to work together and not be divided." But when it comes to acting it out, I frequently fall short without even realizing it. Maybe it goes far deeper than our shallow psyche wants to understand.

I have seen an example of the lack of accepting other puzzle pieces and missing the whole as a result very clearly in a recent situation. My brother is a studier of the word. For years he has loved to study God's word at a level most people do not. It is clearly a gift, and anyone who knows my brother would agree. Not long ago, he began to pray and ask God to show him more clearly how to please his heart. Suddenly, Scripture from the Old Testament began to speak to him in new ways. My brother saw a revolving theme in the Old Testament. God loves the Sabbath, he longs for his people to keep it holy. Yet with the age of grace we have completely thrown it out. He also saw health instructions that modern day followers have thrown out and he has begun to observe those. His explanation is that if you were sick you would go to a health book to find a cure, God's word is our health book for the human body, and the human condition. God did not give the Israelites rules without reason.

As my brother began to speak to others about what he believed God was revealing to him, he was met with ridiculous resistance and closed minded people. He has been judged, insulted, challenged, and shut out by many Christians. Yet my brother has found multiple verses both in Old and New Testaments that back up that God wants us to keep the Sabbath holy, even today.

The response has been so strong that believers that were once friends that respected him began to ostracize him. On many occasions he was called a legalist. Never did he say that God would send anyone to hell if they did not keep the Sabbath, never did he say keeping the Sabbath saved mankind. He was only teaching that keeping the Sabbath pleases God's heart, the same way that telling the truth, or staying faithful to your wife, or keeping any other of the 10 commandments pleases God's heart. An adulterous person will not necessarily go to hell, but it is not pleasing to God, it is disobedient to his commands, and continually doing it when you know it is wrong definitely says something about your heart toward God. I believe that breaking the Sabbath will not cause you to go to hell, but I believe it grieves God's heart that our culture views it as unimportant. You may want to do your own research on this to come to your own conclusion; I am not trying to guilt anyone or teach on the Sabbath. What I am trying to do is give an illustration of how God reveals truth to us all.

Sometimes we shut out what someone else is teaching because God has given us one piece of the puzzle, but our pride keeps us from uniting with other pieces.

I strongly believe there is a purpose for the different understandings and gifting's, particularly those that are extreme opposites. I believe that it is almost a check and balance type of thing, as well as a way God has caused us to need to lean on one another to do his work.

Recently I heard a radio broadcast of controversial content. The man leading the broadcast was speaking boldly about how many people take Scripture out of context. He was absolutely right in what he was saying. He pulled Jeremiah 29:11 out for discussion. It says, ' "For I know the plans I have for you," declares the Lord, "plans to prosper you and not to harm you, plans to give you hope and a future."' According to him, it is wrong for us to use that in any other context except the context in which it was written. Which was specifically to the Jews at that time and generation. Nothing else. According to him it is wrong to use it for today or any other time era. It is historical documentation and nothing else. Yet many people use it for a Scripture for encouragement and promise in modern day. The teacher said that if we are going to use the Scripture to apply to today, then we must also take Jeremiah 26, which speaks of punishment and cursing.

There were some people who called into the show offended at what he was saying. I could understand, I have used this Scripture many times for my own encouragement. But I also kept in mind as I listened that host of the show was not necessarily speaking against the teaching I would take, and he was correct in most of what he was saying. He was calling out the danger in taking this Scripture out of context. Some people use this Scripture as a promise for prosperity, and that is not the case. If that is the "take away" of any teaching on this verse, it is completely out of context. It doesn't even line up with the rest of Scripture. So I agree with his strong stance there. I also agree that the context needs to be remembered. It was originally to the Israelites. I agree that if we take the promise of Jeremiah 29:11 we also must claim Jeremiah 26which speaks of severe consequences for disobedience.

Here is where I did not agree with him. I do believe strongly there is an angle we can use this Scripture to teach us about modern day circumstances. I believe this Scripture tells us a lot about the character of God. If he knew the plans he had for Israel, then I believe he knows the plans he has for America, and more intimately for you and for me. In Jeremiah 26 he talked about destruction for the Israelite's disobedience, I believe that our disobedience will lead to calamity today. God's intent for their destruction was not to ultimately harm them but to bring them to repentance; the same is true if God allows our destruction today. I believe that the calamity is never ultimately for our destruction, but to prosper us. Not in the name of fame or fortune, but as spiritual form of prosperity. There are Scriptures to corroborate everything I interpreted this piece of Scripture to say. There is not Scripture to back up what others may interpret it to be such as the idea that God's going to give financial prosperity. When you look at Jeremiah 29:11 to find God's character, it can be found; he gives consequences for disobedience, but only for repentance and spiritual prosperity, never for calamity. God always has a plan; we should trust him with it.

Instead of weighing the truth this man presented, people were calling vehemently disagreeing with him. They were furious. One woman emailed him to inform him that she had listened to him for years, but those days were gone. The host himself said the response was almost as if he was taking away their God, and in a way he was.

Here is my point-- are we too attached to our own view of God to learn what he may be trying to teach us through another puzzle piece? It is important we look for balance. I'm not saying to be open to everything anyone says. That is dangerous. Remember the chapter about dancing against the enemy? What I am saying is that God's word is complex, and we are simple in our ability to understand it. Sometimes God is praised through jumping and shouting, sometimes through quiet reflection. Neither is only right, neither is wrong. Unless it is a show, then both can be wrong, but it is never for me to judge the motives of someone else's heart. Sometimes God reveals a part of his character to you and sometimes he reveals another part to someone else. We may have extreme differences in our view; in such a case it is my responsibility to seek out God's truth. Perhaps we are in each other's lives to find balance on our extreme viewpoint. We can learn a lot from each other. But the question is, are we willing to? Or is it easier to keep company with others who see the world the exact same way we do?

Three Examples of the Pharisees

The Pharisees were very certain they had things right too. They were closed off to the truth because they knew too much to learn about the truth. They only consulted people who had the same viewpoints as their own and they refused to dig into ancient Scripture to ponder if they were missing something. They were determined they were doing God's will. I have found three examples of Pharisees who thought they had it right. They all have very different endings to their stories and I think we can learn a lot from these examples.

The first example is of those who were directly involved in Christ's crucifixion. Caiaphas himself said it was better for Jesus to die to stop the movement he started then for the whole nation to perish on account of him. They were certain they had the "things of God" figured out, yet they were the ones who were wrong. Likely they all went to their graves lost, deceived and dead wrong. Where did that leave their eternal souls as a result of murdering the Son of God? It is not for us to judge, but wise for us to ponder.

I don't mean it is a good thing to believe everything another Christian says simply because they are Christians, nor do I think that every form of worship is true worship, or every Biblical perspective is right on. However, I think sometimes we can be so stuck on own interpretation of Scripture or religious practices that we miss out on truth. How many times are we missing the full picture because we only have one piece of the puzzle yet refuse to look into others? We too can be dead wrong in our perspective. It is wise to ponder where that may leave our eternal souls.

Saul was another example of a Pharisee who thought he was doing God's will. He was passionate for God, and he was certain he was doing God's work by killing followers of Christ. But he was wrong. It took God knocking him off his horse and a personal reprimanding before he would even consider that he might be wrong. I never want to be there. I never want to be so stuck on my own perspective that I am misleading others. I don't want to be puffed up in my pride, and then knocked off my high horse with consequences that I can't take back either. I'm sure Saul lived with some emotional remorse for his behavior from the days before God knocked him down.

I see this form of fixation in doctrine that talks about baptism for salvation versus a prayer for salvation. Does it matter? Scripture says get baptized when you believe so do it. I don't know that it is important to know exactly when we receive the Holy Spirit.

I have heard apologists and historians argue about if creation was a literal 7 days or if it took thousands or millions of years. Again, does it matter among Christians? Why waste time arguing about creation when Jesus is what is required for salvation.

I see it in Pre tribulation, mid tribulation, and post tribulation theory stances. Does it matter? Be ready when ever he comes, and be ready to suffer.

We don't know all spiritual matters. The thing that got the Pharisees into trouble in both of these examples is that they were too determined they were knew what the Scriptures meant about the coming Messiah that they were blind to the Truth when He showed up. I don't want to box God in. I have, but I don't want to. He is too big, and too mysterious for me to claim to understand. The longer I live, the more I relinquish the need to put God in my own box. He is the God he is, not the God I think He is.

In contrast to the Pharisees who died in their ignorance, and to Saul who had to knocked off his horse and reprimanded by God, there is Nicodemus, who got it right. When all of the other Pharisees had their minds made up about who Jesus was, Nicodemus chose to seek out answers. It is highly probable that he did not like Jesus when he went to him. He may have had opinions about what Jesus was saying and who he was, but rather than staying in his ignorance he sought Jesus out with an open mind to what he may learn. Nicodemus chose to have a direct conversation about what Jesus was teaching. In the end I believe he must have decided that Jesus was right, and the other Pharisees had it wrong.

There is a difference between ignorance and foolishness. Someone may be ignorant of facts, or Biblical truth or understanding. We have no control over those things we are unaware of. But when the chance of learning or understanding presents itself, and we refuse to believe it or even consider it to be truth we are no longer ignorant but foolish.

Let's try learning to dance like Nicodemus. Let's learn to throw out the competition about who is the better Christian, who knows the most, or who is right. There are times where people are teaching blatant false teachings. I am supportive of calling out lies for lies. In fact, please put a stop to teaching that is obviously contrary to God's word. But some things are less clear. Some things may take prayer and consideration. Some things are about finding the correct balance. Always remember that. Again, I never want to be so ridged and strong on my stance that I am closed to hearing others, I may miss out on learning God's truth for me.

Application

One way to fight foolishness is when you are confronted with information that goes against what you believe to be true ask yourself these questions.

Why do I disagree with the interpretation of the Scripture in question?

Is it that I disagree with what this person says the Scripture means or is it that I don't like what this person says the Scripture means?

On the other hand to avoid conflict as you state your view you can always turn the question around.

Why do you disagree with the interpretation of the Scripture in question?

Is it that you disagree that this is what the Scripture means or is it that you don't like it?

*(1) Sourced in back

"God is God and I am not, I can only see a part of the picture He painting and God is God and I am man, so I'll never understand it all for only God is God." ~Steven Curtis Chapman, God is God

"I cling to you. Your right arm holds me up." Psalm 68:3

"Whatever my lot thou hast taught me to say it is well with my soul." ~It is Well

"You are still Holy, even when I don't understand your ways. Sovereign, you are still Sovereign, even when my circumstances don't change." ~Rita Springer, You are Still Holy

Chapter 15
Dancing in Total Security

The title of this chapter is "Dancing in Total Security", but quite honestly it just as easily could have been "Complete Surrender". Though they are very different in this physical world we live in, they are one in the same in the Christian world. As Christians we are completely safe, securely held in the arms of our maker, yet we don't realize that we are secure, and so we wrestle with God.

You may be a little confused about that first paragraph in reference to what I wrote earlier in this book. You may be saying at this point "Wait a minute, I thought you said it is good to wrestle with God? Now you are saying if we are walking the way we should we don't wrestle?" Well yes, and no. It is human to wrestle. It is wise to wrestle sometimes, but there comes a time when wrestling must stop and we have to decide to trust God. This is not necessarily a onetime thing, but it may be more of a lifetime process as situations arise. Hopefully each time we are faced with a wrestling match with God it becomes easier to surrender to Him, rather than digging into our determination to get answers.

My mom says that each of us has a besetting sin. I agree with her, each of us has a tendency to struggle with some things that others may not and vice versa. My mom has told me that she believes mine is impatience, and though I can agree there was a time I was very impatient, I believe that these days I am more patient than most. My big sin is that I wrestle. I don't mean the healthy kind of wrestling that I mentioned earlier in this book, I mean that I get so bold that I am up in God's face with my fists balled up screaming "but why God??" all the while refusing to relent until I have a satisfactory answer. I wrestle with God more than anyone I know. This kind of wrestling is sinful, and untrusting; yet God has been patient with me.

The other day I was praying intensely to God as I was doing yard work. It was a very intense conversation with God and I was wrestling with him again, about something we had settled. "God I understand this is how you want things, and I am thankful for how things are, I really am. But what I don't understand is why…I don't think that is how things should be, it doesn't seem fair to me."

Suddenly I felt a very intense reprimand from the Holy Spirit shoot back at me, "That is not your business." Again, let me say, this was not the first time I wrestled with God on this particular subject. I was still questioning God's wisdom even after years of wrestling, and a very long process where the period was clearly put on the situation, yet I decided to open it up for discussion again. After the holy reprimand, I undoubtedly quickly shut my mouth and went back to raking.

Since that day I began to confess to God my besetting sin of questioning him, and wrestling. My book, my talent of singing, my love to teach his word, my hour drive to work and back, my job, my hopes and dreams for my future. All of them have been laid down at the feet of Jesus, and when I am tempted to pick them back up, I say "Your will and Yours alone God, my future is not my business, and if all of my talents are left to waste, it will be in obedience to you for your glory. Let me learn what you say my purpose for this life is. I am finally learning total security, and total surrender. This is the goal in our Christian walk.

God desires that we would long to learn how to walk through life feeling that we are securely in His arms no matter what life throws at us.

Another way of explaining security is to say that we feel safe and trusting enough to surrender our will to God. We no longer fight him, we no longer wrestle, we no longer question, we simply say "You know what your doing. I have faith in you. I'm jumping in, no questions asked. Whatever happens is of you, I trust you."

Dancing the Dance of life with Christ in total security is not unlike the story of Charles Blondon and his manager. Blondon was a tight ropewalker in the mid to late 1800's. He walked across Niagara Falls on a tight rope. To make things interesting he began to do several different tricks such as ride a bike across the falls, or push a wheelbarrow. His grace and talent drew people from miles. Then one day he asked the crowd how many people thought he could successfully walk the tight rope with a man on his back. The crowd went crazy with support, until he asked who was willing to volunteer. Not one person was willing to risk their life to trust him with it, but they were all willing to cheer him on, they were willing to verbalize their support. It was one thing to trust him with someone else's life, but completely different to trust him with theirs.

Eventually Blondon's manager committed to be the one to trust Blondon with his life, and successfully they made it across the falls. What would have happened if the manager began kicking and flailing around on the back of the Blondon as he was carrying him hundreds of feet above the falls? How long would they be on course? How smooth would it be? Would they even make it to the destination?

Many people talk a good talk about God, but how many people are really willing to get up on the back of Christ and let him carry them over the scary falls of life? How many will surrender, close their eyes, sit still, and trust him enough to securely let him carry them across the turmoil of their life? Perhaps the time that this is hardest is during trials, but it is during the trials in life we have the potential to be refined the most. Notice, I said potential. When God allows a trial, that is exactly what his purpose is, to refine you. But we can buck God, we can become bitter at life, we may reject what he is doing in us. This is not dancing in total security.

How Learning to Dance with Security Changes Us

I can look over my life and see trials, some that I brought on myself, and some God has brought into my life, I can acknowledge the suffering. But I can also see how has God has healed and refined me in my suffering. James 1:2-4 says "Consider it pure joy my brothers, when you go through trials of many kinds, because you know the testing of your faith develops perseverance. Perseverance must finish its work so that you may be mature and complete, not lacking in anything." We grow in our struggles, if we let God do his work in us. 1 Peter 4:1 says "Therefore since Christ suffered in his body, arm yourselves also with the same attitude, because he who suffers in his body is done with sin. As a result he does not live the rest of his life for evil human desires, but rather for the will of God." Suffering can refine us, but there is a choice we have when trials and suffering faces us. We can allow God to refine us, or we may become bitter through the trial. Dancing with security ensures refinement leading to a better version of ourselves.

I remember the day some unkind words that had been said about me came back to me ears. I was taken by surprise at how much the mean spirited words did not hurt me, but instead stirred up compassion for the lost soul who had uttered them. This response did not come naturally. This response came after years of learning how to forgive, how to love my enemy, and how to look to my Father in heaven for my value rather than to other people. In other words this response came from years of trials that have taught me to rest securely in the arms of Jesus even when I want to retaliate, or act in some unkind way.

This kind of security brings peace in many situations. Rather than hate and anger, there is peace. Rather than fear and anxiety, there is peace. Rather than a need for control, there is peace. No matter what the circumstances; relational, financial, marital, work related, health related when we face trials of any kind, we can be at peace knowing that God has allowed the trial, and he is doing a work for change from the inside out.

How Dancing in security can change us.

There's another beauty that comes in dancing in total security through trials. In May of 2015, a man by the name of Jonathan McComb from Corpus Christie, Texas went of vacation with his family and some friends to Wimberley, Texas over Memorial Day weekend. Severe storms hit the area while they were there; leading to deadly flooding. At one point during this family vacation the home they were staying in was swept off the foundation and down the river. In this tragedy Jonathan lost everything that he held dear. In the flood, Jonathan's wife, two children and friends that were in the house all died, leaving Jonathan the lone survivor and terribly traumatized.

If anyone had the right to question God, Jonathan would be it. If anyone had a reason to become bitter, or curl up in a ball and give up it would be Jonathon. But instead Jonathon is leading others to Christ, inspiring others to grow in their relationship with Christ, and others are coming back to Christ because of his example of dancing in total security with Christ through this tragedy.

Jonathan has publically spoken about his peace with God over this tragedy. I cannot put into words better than Jonathan himself so I will let you read it directly from a usurp taken from the article written by Julie Garcia*(1) with quotes from Jonathan himself:

> "Remembering back to that fateful night, McComb said he didn't pull himself out of the river — God did that.
> "It wasn't me. It was Him helping push me," he said.
> "For what reason, I don't know. Maybe it's for me to let people know that there is hope and faith, and there's no

reason to get discouraged. Sometimes life is tough. It's hard. But you need to stay focused on the Lord and everything else. He'll get you through it. I hope that message spreads like wildfire."

His story is not the miracle, he said. "I'm the mailman. There's a good thing that comes out of tragedy, and I know that Laura, Andrew and Leighton would be ecstatic to know they're a part of it." (1)

When we go through trails or difficulties the world is watching us. Tragedies in our lives are the perfect times for us to show the world the difference of living as the rest of the world or living as a Christian. God sometimes allows tragedies to bring others to himself. If we throw tantrums, become bitter, or become hardened we hurt our witness. But if we can be secure and surrender to God, we have the potential to make a big impact on this world.

Of course this is not easy. It may take years of learning to dance with Christ before you can dance as beautifully through tragedy as he has. You may even find that it is easier to dance in security on some days than others. But keeping the big picture in mind during the dance is a beautiful thing.

Mary the mother of Jesus faced a very interesting dance of security. When the angel came to her and talked with her about the plan, she knew she was facing ridicule. She knew people would not believe her. She knew she could be facing severe consequences of having an unwed pregnancy, especially while engaged to a man who knew he was not the father; and yet her response was, "Behold, I am the servant of the Lord. May it be to me according to your word." Luke 1:38.

Finding strength in Scripture

Psalm 112:4-6 says that a man who is upright will never be shaken. Job 11:18 reminds us that we are to feel secure even in struggles because there is hope. Psalm 46 reminds us that God is our strength and refuge. He is always present in our times of trouble. Jesus promises in John 14 that we will face troubles of many kinds in this broken world, but we are to take heart because Jesus has overcome the world. He is bigger than anything this world dishes out. So when those troubles come our way, the best thing we can do is cling to Christ, rest in his arms as he gracefully twirls us across the tight rope of life. If we fight it or try to take control it will be a much longer, harder, dance than if we rest in his grip and allow his right arm to hold us up (Psalm 68:3).

*(1) Sourced in back

*"If the Son sets you free you will be
free indeed." ~ John 8:36*

*"Where the spirit of the Lord is there is freedom, Lift your
eyes to heaven, there is freedom…Freedom reigns in this
place, showers of mercy and Grace falling on every face,
there is freedom." ~ Jesus Culture; Freedom Reigns*

Chapter 16
Dancing In Freedom

This book may have seemed like it was heavy, and in some ways I completely agree. But here is the good news. Saying yes to the dance of life with Christ is saying yes to freedom. Galatians 4:8 points out that before we came to Christ we were slaves to things that in their nature are not God. Even Jesus in John 8:36 says that anyone who sins is a slave to sin. We become slaves to our desires, comforts and longings. But when we begin to dance with Christ he sets us free.

We are all slaves to something Romans 6:16-18 says we can be slaves to righteousness, which gives freedom, or slaves to sin, which is bondage. Those who are not in Christ are slaves to their lustful desires. The wife of their youth did not fulfill, so they go in search of a new wife who fulfills for a time…until she doesn't anymore. Sexual desires cry out, demanding to be satisfied and soon a road of broken relationships follow. Heterosexual relationships don't satisfy, so they try out homosexual satisfaction, which also leaves them longing for more. Nights of drinking past the fill, leaves people empty, embarrassed and hung over in the morning. Stuffing and gorging on food until it feels like you will explode leaves you feeling sick, lazy and sluggish, not to mention hungry again for more soon after. No amount of riches or status is ever enough. Those left to their own standards to find satisfaction spend their lives seeking yet not finding.

Those who are lukewarm are even worse. Revelation says that God will spit out those who are lukewarm. Besides that fact that God finds lukewarm Christianity detestable, Christians who are on the fence feel stuck in the middle. They seek fleshy gratification, yet they have a conscious. The morning after feels worse because deep inside they know they are hurting themselves and hurting God. There is a ripping in the spirit that happens if you are lukewarm. 1 John 2:15-16 says you cannot be friends of this world and friends with God. You will either follow his teaching or you will follow what the world says, very rarely do the two line up congruently.

Matthew 6 and Luke 16 both talk about our inability to serve two masters. In context it is talking about how we cannot serve God and love money, however I would dare to say this is true of anything. We cannot fully love the Lord and be liars, we cannot fully be committed to God and have an addiction to too much wine or some other substance. We cannot fully serve God and carry lust in our hearts. It is impossible to give all of our hearts to God, and keep a part of it away from him at the same time. Trying to balance this is destructive to our lives, our families, and our soul. In the end it may be God we end up hating.

But when you dance the dance of life with Christ, you are free. Free from the slavery and bondage of your every desire. Romans 6:11-14 says that those who live in Christ do not allow sin to reign in their mortal body. We will still sin, but we will also be free from the addictions that once ran our lives. You will be free from the guilt of knowing you are offending a holy God. Yoking up with Christ is satisfying to the deepest places of the soul. He fills longings, he breaks the addictions, and he frees us from our neuroticism that leads to so many mental health disorders. He frees us from guilt. He gives us a safe place to fall. He helps us learn how to forgive, which frees us from the burning pain of hate, resentment, and bitterness. He helps us to have grace for others and ourselves when we don't get it right.

We may not be totally free from everything at once, but as we learn new dances and get better at following his lead there is a beauty we will possess that others will not have. We won't need to hang on to our pride. We won't need to control others; we won't need to have things our way because we are clinging to the one who has conquered death. Anxiety will be diminished because we will understand we have nothing to fear. Depression will subside to some extent because his light will shine on situations that felt so black before. We will spin, and twirl, and leap in complete freedom, even during the hardest dances. Letting go of the empty lies of this world is worth it when you are participating in the dance of life with Christ.

To The Steadfast Believer

If you are already doing the best you can in the dance with Christ, I urge you to go deeper. He will teach you as many dances as you are willing to let him. He will continue to teach and refine you all of your life, but you must be willing to learn. Ask him to take you deeper, and then follow his steps as he urges you to learn what it means to go deeper.

To The Luke Warm Believer

If you have accepted Christ, but you are recognizing that you have not fully committed to the dance, I urge you to begin to change your own steps. Those silly things you chase after will always let you down. They do not satisfy, not for long anyway. When I was beginning my dance, I remember recognizing that "happiness was always around the next corner."

> I thought I'd be happy when...
> When I got a wardrobe of nice clothes
> When I had had the money to buy better face care products
> When I had a boyfriend
> When I had more money
> When I fit in with others

I never was. Those things were nice, but I wanted more. More money, more clothes, to get married, for my husband to change, to have more things, to look more like Barbie…whatever. Jesus satisfies. Don't be afraid to let go of the world, her promises are empty lies. Besides that nothing hurts more than straddling the line. Either reject Christ and live your life in complete blindness, or commit. But for your own sake don't straddle the line. It torments.

To The Seeker

If you have never accepted Christ I urge you to make a commitment. Romans says it is an unveiling of our eyes that draws us to him. If you are seeing something new please don't harden your heart to that. Know he is personally calling to you. Respond to him today. Pray, let him know you hear him and you accept him. Tell him about your sin. Tell him specifics. Ask him to cleanse you. Ask him to become Lord of your life, and then ask him to teach you what steps you need to learn first. When I first entered my dance, I would pray face down telling God what I was not able to give up yet. He taught me how to give it up over time. He taught me new steps over several years. I did what I could, and confessed what I was unable to change in that moment. He doesn't expect us to be fixed when we come to him; he just wants you authentically broken.

Lord,

I pray for all of my readers. I ask that you have used me, this very broken vessel, to speak your truth into their lives. Lord, please meet each person where he/she is. Please teach all of us how to dance new and better dances with you. May the seed of your Word and truth in this book not return void.

Amen

Appendix I

Resources for Further Research

From Chapter 2

Bible City Forum, Krauss, L.& William Lane Craig. (2013, September 3). Life the universe and nothing: Has science buried God? Debate facilitated by the Bible City Forum. Video retrieved from http://www.richarddawkins.net/news_articles/2013/9/2/life-the-universe-and-nothing-has-science-buried-god?videos=true#

C. Meister. (2006).Building Belief: Constructing From the Ground Up. Grand Rapids, Michigan. Baker Books

C. Meister. (2006).Building Belief: Constructing From the Ground Up. Grand Rapids, Michigan. Baker Books

Dawkins, R. (2012) The God dilusion. Retrieved from http://youtu.be/9FiHRVb_uE0

Dawkins, R. (2012) The God dilusion. Retrieved from http://youtu.be/9FiHRVb_uE0

Illustra Media. (2009). Darwin's Dilema

Illustra Media. (2009). Darwin's Dilema

Strobel, L. Allen, W.P., Eaton, M. (Writers).Eaton, M., Eaton, T. (Directors). Allen, L., Bueno, C., Frenzel, L., Harned, J. (Producers). (2007) Case for Christ.LaMirada Films.[DVD].

Strobel, L. Allen, W.P., Eaton, M. (Writers).Eaton, M., Eaton, T. (Directors). Allen, L., Bueno, C., Frenzel, L., Harned, J. (Producers). (2006). The Case for a Creator.Illustra Media. [DVD].

Strobel, L. Allen, W.P., Eaton, M. (Writers).Eaton, M., Eaton, T. (Directors). Allen, L., Bueno, C., Frenzel, L., Harned, J. (Producers). (2007) Case for Christ.LaMirada Films.[DVD].

Strobel, L. Allen, W.P., Eaton, M. (Writers).Eaton, M., Eaton, T. (Directors). Allen, L., Bueno, C., Frenzel, L., Harned, J. (Producers).

(2006). The Case for a Creator. Illustra Media. [DVD].

Lewic, C.S. (1952). Mere Christianity. MacMillian, Co

Limbaugh, D. (2015). The Emmaus Code; Finding Jesus in the Old Testament. Regnery Publishing. Washington DC.

McDowell, J. (1981). The Resurrection Factor: Does Historicl Evidence Support the Ressurection of Christ? Nashville, Tennessee. Thomas Nelson Publishers.

McDowell, J. (1981). The Resurrection Factor: Does Historicl Evidence Support the Ressurection of Christ? Nashville, Tennessee. Thomas Nelson Publishers.

McDowell, J. (1998). The New Evidence That Demands a Verdict (1&2). Thomans Nelson Publishers. Nashville.

McDowell, J. (1998). The New Evidence That Demands a Verdict (1&2). Thomans Nelson Publishers. Nashville.

Miller, K., Stein, B. (Writers). Frankowski, N. (Director) Craft, L., Ruloft, W., Sullivan, J. (Producers). (2008). Expelled: No Intelligence Allowed. [DVD]

Miller, K., Stein, B. (Writers). Frankowski, N. (Director) Craft, L., Ruloft, W., Sullivan, J. (Producers). (2008). Expelled: No Intelligence Allowed. [DVD]

Wiester, J. (1983). The Genesis Connection. Thomas Nelson, Inc. Nashville, Tennisee.

Wiester, J. (1983). The Genesis Connection. Thomas Nelson, Inc. Nashville, Tennisee.

Also, check out *Cross Examined*'s website and podcast.

Appendix II

Learn to Apply Concepts from this Book

Our culture does not do well with teaching us how to navigate through difficult times with patience, trust, and wisdom. Many mental health professionals are beginning to be aware of this deficit in our culture and they have begun to teach what is referred to as emotional regulation skills. As I have studied these techniques, I have been able to see the Biblical substance and wisdom in them as well. At an extreme level some of these techniques can become "New Age-ish". But at a foundational level, these techniques are Biblical.

I have pulled information for this section from therapies such as Dialectical Behavioral Therapy (DBT), Acceptance Commitment Therapy (ACT), and Mindfulness discipline (learning to be present in the moment and paying attention). By applying these concepts and combining them with a Biblical mind-set you can more easily learn how to "dance through the storms of life, wait on hope, and fight against the dead man dancing". Anytime you are faced with discomfort, these concepts can be applied. These concepts can also be applied when there is no crisis, or discomfort. Apply these as a way of worship, self-examination/reflection, or meditating on God.

Some Scriptural Support

James 1:19	Proverbs 17:27-28	Proverbs 4:23
Philippians 4:6-7	2 Corinthians 4:4	1 Peter 1:13
Mark 7:21	Philippians 4:8	Mark 7:20-22
Romans 12:2	Philippians 2:2-8	Romans 8:5-7
Psalm 62:1	Psalm 46:10	Psalm 5:3
Zephaniah 3:17	Psalm 37:37	Psalm 19:14
Psalm 1:2	Psalm 4:4	Psalm 143:5

The acronym S.T.O.P. may help you remember the steps.

S. Slow your breathing. You can do this where you are, but it may also help to go to a quiet place. Remind yourself that your breath is fragile (James 4:14-15), Remember that as you breathe in, you are breathing in life and as you exhale you are giving life. Thank God for your life. Be aware that you are fearfully and wonderfully made (Psalm 139), and you were bought with a price (1 Corinthians 6:20)

T. Think. Notice what you are experiencing. Slow yourself down and think about what you are feeling, thinking. What emotions are present? Where are you feeling the emotions? What are the aspects of this situation that you may not be immediately thinking about (what the other person may be experiencing from you, what conclusions are you jumping to, what are you trying to control that you may have no control over)

O. Open Up. Open up to accepting your feelings. Open up to accepting that your situation is what it is. As hard as it is, as painful as it is, as much as you may hate it, you cannot change it immediately or fully. You have limited control. Allow the weight of your emotions and situation to press onto you. Take breaths to allow those feelings to happen. Learn to stop resisting. Pray in this moment. Ask God to come into those feelings, the situation, the fears. Do not hold onto feelings, do not push away feelings, just let them be. Remember that emotions are a gift from God, even the ones that don't feel good. Ask yourself, and the Holy Spirit to reveal to you what is behind the feelings. The heart of man is deceitful above all things, sometimes we are not initially truthful with ourselves about our situations. Sit with your emotions for a while. Honor your emotions, even if you want them to be different. Even if you feel they are wrong, God knows the truth in your emotions (John2:25; Psalm 139). God cannot give healing or wisdom to you if you will not be honest before him, be authentic and acknowledge they are there. Confess sinful thoughts and desires.

P. Pursue your values. It can be easy to fill a void, or ease pain in ways that don't represent our values. Running out to find a lover in order to fill a void, drinking, throwing an angry tantrum relieves initially, but we can look back in shame when we rush to "fix" things. Instead be deliberate about your actions. What do you want people to see in you? When you look back at this moment what do you want to see? What would the best version of you do in this situation? What choices would please God? Look up Scripture that apply to your situation. Do not make any moves until you take a time out to plan your response to this situation whether it is an intense emotion, or a relational situation, or a life crisis. Just wait, plan and be deliberate. Breathe, pray, ask God for wisdom (James 1:5; Proverbs 29:11.)

Questions to ask yourself as you S.T.O.P

- Is this too big for me to figure out alone? Should I ask friends, family, a pastor, or a professional to help me sort this out?

- What ways do I have control over this situation? In what ways am I trying to control when I have no control?

- What can I do in this moment to ease this situation? What can I do in the future to ease this situation?

- What are my fears around those steps? How can I bring my trust in God into this?

- What do I need to do to stay healthy in this moment?

- For those areas where I cannot do anything, how do I learn to "bend like a palm tree?" How do I accept the situation and look for attitudes or steps to help me be spiritually healthy?

- Take blame out of the situation, and ask, "what is my responsibility here?" What steps do you need to take to be humble and make things right?

- Russ Harris says we all get dealt a hand of cards, but we have no control over the hand we receive. Remind yourself you have the hand you have been dealt, so how do you play this hand the best way possible? What strengths already exist to help here? What opportunities are there to build new strengths in this situation? Specifically what strengths do you want to build?

- Assess similar situations in the past. What have you done

well, what can you improve this time around? How will you make those improvements?

- Show yourself compassion. Remember that God does. If this were someone else's storm, what wisdom would you show to them? What wisdom can you find in Scripture for this situation?

After Care

It is natural to ruminate on difficult situations, but it is never helpful. When you find yourself ruminating speak to yourself, out loud if necessary (I find it necessary). Name your emotion "I'm feeling sad again." "Ouch, there's that hurt coming up again." Then begin to remind yourself about the truths of your situation, or reasons for change, or what ever it is that you need to be reminded of.

Example 1
Financial crisis.

"Oh my goodness, I am worrying about paying next months bills again. It is natural to feel anxiety about this, but Michele, you aren't late yet. You very well may be able to pay those bills on time. Stop letting tomorrows worries rob you of today's peace. Remember what Matthew 6:34 says? Instead I will try to keep my focus on the fact that Scripture promises that my God will supply my needs. I will be present in today, and do my best to plan my financial choices in such a way that I can pay my bills on time"

Example 2
Relational Crisis

"I just have to say out loud that I am sad. It hurts when I think about the ways I felt betrayed. I will not get hooked into letting my mind stay here though. I want to focus on the dreams I have for my future, I cannot control where this relationship will go, and I don't want to. Lord, You promise that you have plans for my life according to Jeremiah 29:11. I trust that you only have my best interest at heart, so if this is over I need to accept it and say to you that I do not want to manipulate you, or my friend. That will never work. I am sad, it doesn't feel good, but that is okay. Everyone hurts and right now is my time to hurt."

Appendix III

Extra Writings

This is some of the left over writing that I ended up cutting from the book. I decided to include it in the back so the truth can still be gleaned from it.

Hiding from our real feelings is nothing new. It has been something humans have done from the very beginning of time. When Adam and Eve first sinned what did they do? They thought they were hiding from God. Of course they weren't hiding anything, but they thought they were. And don't we still do the same thing sometimes? There are areas I will readily confess to God, but then there are uglier sides of me that I refuse to look at. I will nod and shake my head in agreement at church thinking how wise I am for already having the understanding the pastor is teaching about patience. I hope against all hope that my husband is listening so he will hear about what I already know. I have not been patient at all with him as he is learning how to be patient.

Why is it that we hide so often? Again, we can boil it down to the exact reason that the first humans first sinned. We don't trust God, or we want more, or we want control of our own lives.

"Trust in the Lord and you will never be disappointed." Now, I have searched the Scriptures and I have not found anything that backs this statement up anywhere, yet I have heard this idea and several similar ones circulated in teachings, Christian conversation, and written work. What I have found in Scripture is an understanding that there will always be mystery; I will face heartache disappointment, struggles, discipline (both for correction, and simply for purposes of growth) and pain. Christ himself said, "on this earth you will face trouble, but take heart, I have overcome the world." (John 16:33)

So where do so many people get this idea that there is no disappointment? I believe it is Scripture that is sprinkled with a little human sugar coating. We want comfort and easy. The above example may specifically refer to the Scripture in Psalm?? Which says "Delight yourself in the Lord and HE will give you the desire of your heart." It is easy to think this is a formula to get what you want, but delighting yourself in the Lord for the purpose to get what you want goes against Scripture. God cannot be mocked or manipulated. What I believe this Scripture is saying that if we find delight in God, our desire for him will increase and God will give us that increase.

How does the above relate to inauthenticity? I have at times found myself doing good in order that I may get the blessing. I coat selfish prayers in words that sound honorable and holy, but my motives are to get God to give to me. This is a dance of inauthenticity and it gets in the way of a genuine exchange with God. It also keeps me in bondage of deceit to myself where I do not see my true motives. I also look great to others in the process. All the while living a guarded, manipulative, pretense of a Christian life. It also sets me up for disappointment.

Another way we are inauthentic is when we refuse to look at our hurts or disappointments, failures or how our past may be affecting us. Good Christian people don't live in the past. After all it is Scriptural. I Cortinthians 5:17 says "I'm a new creation the old things have past away." And Philippians 3:13 says, "Forgetting what is behind I press on toward the goal to win the prize for which God has called me heavenward." It is Scriptural to leave the past in the past. So how is that being inauthentic?

Well, if my past is affecting my now, but I keep putting it up on the shelf in my heart then I am being inauthentic. Let me see if I can clarify it for you. I am a runner. I love to run 4, 5, and even sometimes 6 miles at a time. When I was 15 years old I broke my ankle. That wound happened 22 years ago, I wore a cast for 3 months and eventually I was able to walk on it again. The trauma is long behind me. However, every now and then the old wound of the past sneaks up on me. If it happens when I'm walking, let alone running, I have to stop and care for that old wound before I can press on any further. Sometimes caring for it simply means limping for a few steps. Sometimes it means stopping and rotating it in one direction and then in the other for a couple minutes. Once I have cared for it, I can continue to press forward. If a pain, or disappointment is affecting you today, it is not in your past. The only way to clear it up is to be authentic about the pain, take it off the shelf and take it before God and ask him to unpack the pain, and disappointment.

In 1 John 3:18-20 (make sure) it says, "Dear children let us not love with words or tongue but with action and in TRUTH. This then is how we know we belong to the TRUTH, and how we set our hearts at rest in his presence whenever our hearts condemn us. For God is greater than our hearts, and He knows everything."

When we walk in truth, we can have confidence that God will see truth. I believe that what this Scripture is saying is take off the masks walk in truth. When you see your sinful nature you are in truth, and your heart may condemn itself, but God sees the truth. He sees the truth that I am a corrupt human being, unable to walk in perfection. He sees the truth of the heart he created in me.

We need to walk in truth, and walking in truth means not putting on a façade in front of others, God or ourselves. We man fool others, or ourselves, we will never fool God. But God is a gentleman.

He will not go into anything we don't invite him into. But if we don't invite him into our genuine heart our disappointments with him, our anger at him or others, our sin…then it festers and becomes an infection.

    Life gives us wounds. Sometimes it's because we did something to ourselves, like my son who jumped out of a moving vehicle. Sometimes it is not our choices, like a car accident where someone else made the choice to drink and drive, sometimes choice has nothing to do with it, like when we are faced with cancer. But if we praise God, trust him, and refuse to take those questions of our hearts to him, we are doing nothing but ignoring a wound that will fester into infection. It will affect healthy tissue. It will affect our perception in life. We may go to our grave without addressing the infection, but we will not be unaffected by ignoring it

Citations

Chapter 2

Bible City Forum, Krauss, L.& William Lane Craig. (2013, September 3). Life the universe and nothing: Has science buried God? Debate facilitated by the Bible City Forum. Video retrieved from http://www.richarddawkins.net/news_articles/2013/9/2/life-the-universe-and-nothing-has-science-buried-god?videos=true#

Chapter 3

Lliades, C (2013) "Stats and Facts about Depression in America". Everyday Health. Retrieved from: http://www.everydayhealth.com/health-report/major-depression/depression-statistics.aspx

Parker-Pope, T. (2013). New York Times

James, Carolyn Custis. When Life and Beliefs Collide: How Knowing God Makes a Difference. Grand Rapids, MI: ZondervanPublishingHouse, 2001. Print.

Smedes, Lewis B. Sex for Christians: The Limits and Liberties of Sexual Living. Grand Rapids: Eerdmans, 1976. Print.

Lewis, C. S. The Lion the Witch and the Wardrobe. New York, NY: Macmillian, 1950. Print

Chapter 4

Crabb, Larry. Shattered Dreams. Colorado Springs, CO: Waterbrook Press, 2001. Print

James, Carolyn Custis. When Life and Beliefs Collide: How Knowing God Makes a Difference. Grand Rapids, MI: ZondervanPublishingHouse, 2001. Print.

Chapter 5

DeGroat, Chuck. Leaving Egypt: Finding God in the Wilderness Places. Grand Rapids, MI: Square Inch, 2011. Print.

Chapter 6

Warren, Rick (2015). The Storms; Three Reasons Why People Get Themselves Into A Mess. Faith Gateway. Retrieved from: http://www.faithgateway.com/storms-of-life-the-anchor-of-god/#.VtWX9se4lxh

Chapter 7

Fenelon, F. The Seeking Heart; The Library of Spiritual Classis (Vol 4). Sargent, GA: The SeedSowers Christian Publishing House

Chapter 8

Schultz, Tammy, and Hannah Estabrook. Beyond Desolate: Hope versus Hate in the Rubble of Sexual Abuse. Winona Lake, IN: BMH, 2012. Print.

Chapter 9

The Tourist. Dir. Florin Henckel Von Donnersmarck. Perf. Jonny Depp, Angelina Jolie. Sony, 2010. DVD.

(https://www.barna.org/barna-update/article/12-faithspirituality/260-most-american-christians-do-not-believe-that-satan-or-the-holy-spirit-exis#.VF1P7Uu4klI)

Michaelsen, Johanna. The Beautiful Side of Evil. Eugene, Or: Harvest House, 1982. Print.

The Lion King. Walt Disney Studios, 1994. DVD.

Chapter 11

McDonald, James. Walk in the Word. http://www.jamesmacdonald.com

Woodsmall, Cindy. The Bridge of Peace: An Ada's House Novel. Colorado Springs, CO: WaterBrook, 2010. Print.

Moore, Beth. When Godly People Do Ungodly Things: Arming Yourself in the Age of Seduction. Nashville, TN: Broadman & Holman, 2002. Print.

Chapter 12

Lucado. M. (1996). The Grip of Grace. Nashville, TN: Thomas Nelson.

Chapter 13

Jeremiah, D. (2007). Hope; An anchor for life. Turning Point

Chapter 14

http://www.caller.com/news/local/wimberley-flood-survivor-jonathan-mccomb-finds-savior-in-corpus-christi-native-22c686ae-53c1-5d8d-e0-336659011.html